Penny's Picks: 50 Movies
by
Women Filmmakers

Reviews written by
Jan Lisa Huttner
(2002-2011)

Cover design by Melissa A. Wilks

Logos for FF2 Media and WomenArts
also by Melissa A. Wilks

Printed and bound in the United States of America

FF2 Media
(www.films42.com)

TABLE OF CONTENTS

Foreword by
Martha Richards of WomenArts

For almost a decade Jan Lisa Huttner has been writing passionate film reviews from a feminist perspective. When I first encountered her work in 2005, she and her husband Rich were writing reviews for their website, *Films for Two: The Online Guide for Busy Couples*. They would go to films together and then they would each write their own reviews. It was always fun to see what they agreed and disagreed on, and also, the juxtaposition of their reviews underscored the point that women and men can often watch the same film and see something totally different.

Much of Jan's work has been driven by her desire to make sure that women audience members understand that their responses to films are valid and that they have power as consumers. In order to understand the bravery and importance of this work, you need to understand the astonishing pervasiveness of gender discrimination in the feature film world.

Recent studies have shown that men write and/or direct approximately 90% of the major Hollywood films and also men write the overwhelming majority of film reviews in the nation's top newspapers. This means that most of the female characters we see on screen are a product of men's imaginations, and most of the reviews we see are male responses to these male-created characters. Many male reviewers never seem to notice when the female characters are under-developed or totally unrealistic, and when they review films that focus on women characters and their perspectives, they tend to dismiss them as "chick flicks."

Jan's voice is a refreshing challenge to these male assessments, and since 2007, I have been delighted to publish her reviews on the WomenArts website. In this book she has gathered fifty of her reviews of films written and/or directed by women. Many of these films have memorable female characters, and it is wonderful to learn more about them.

As Jan has pointed out in countless blog posts and lectures, women have a lot of untapped box office power. Hollywood is driven by profits, and if we can show that there is a large paying audience for films by and about women, then producers will be interested in making more of those films.

As a way of mobilizing women as film consumers, Jan helped found WITASWAN (Women in the Audience Supporting Women Artists Now). WITASWAN is an entirely volunteer grassroots movement of women who make a pledge to see at least one film written and/or directed by a woman every month, either in a theatre, on DVD, or online. Usually women take the pledge with several friends so that they can talk about the films they see.

Ever since the idea was announced in 2004, WITASWAN groups have been springing up around the U.S. Please feel free to start your own group! This collection of Jan's reviews will be a great place to find women's films to watch with your friends.

In 2007, Jan and I declared a new international holiday called **Support Women Artists Now Day** (or **International SWAN Day** for short). I don't think I ever would have done something that bold without the inspiration of Jan's passion, energy, and chutzpah. We sparked each other, and then International SWAN Day captured the imaginations of women around the world. In the past four years there have now been over 700 SWAN events in 21 countries, involving thousands of artists and audience members every year! SWAN Day is a terrific example of what can happen when women start talking to each other about our true feelings and concerns.

I hope that you enjoy these reviews, and that Jan's unique voice and perspective will inspire you as much as they have inspired me.

Martha Richards
Executive Director
WomenArts

Create. Connect. Change the World.

Introducing *Penny's Picks*

When a tree falls in the forest...?

Welcome to *Penny's Picks,* a compilation of reviews of movies by women filmmakers published between 2002 and 2011.

As I explain in my two "historical background" presentations, I first encountered the term "Celluloid Ceiling" on June 2, 2002, while peacefully reading the Arts & Leisure section of my Sunday *New York Times.* Believe me, when I woke up that morning, I had no idea my life was about to change, but change it did, and now, almost ten years later, smashing through the "Celluloid Ceiling" has become one of my lifetime goals.

What accounts for the lack of movies by women filmmakers in the multiplex? When Dana Kennedy wrote her article "An Inpatient Sisterhood" (the article I read that fateful Sunday morning), she quickly invoked the "blame the victim" hypothesis:

> "Are these women suffering from discrimination? Many of them believe they are, but as is so often the case the truth is more complicated than that. Some women in Hollywood, like female politicians and corporate executives, choose to interrupt their careers to have children."

In short, according to Kennedy, if more women would commit themselves to filmmaking, then there would be more films by women filmmakers, and more multiplexes would have more films to offer to their audiences. Problem solved!

But not only is this argument offensive (to female politicians and corporate executives, not to mention female astronauts and soldiers, and women everywhere who successfully juggle multiple roles everyday), it also rests on a totally false assumption.

As readers of this compilation will quickly discover, many, many wonderful films written and/or directed by women have been released in the past decade. Despite all the obstacles, many women have, in fact, completed their films; that is not the problem. The films are there, but what's missing is the audience.

Reasons why women filmmakers are underrepresented in the multiplex include bad marketing, limited rollout, and poor reception from film critics who are disproportionately male. These factors, when combined, typically result in poor performance at the box office. So every time women purchase theatre tickets, their actions have enormous economic consequences. The revenue generated (or not generated) by films directed and/or written by women affects future options for these specific filmmakers as well as all the other women on the team (in front of the camera as well as behind it).

Most women in the audience still don't realize the impact of their decisions. How often have I been told: "There's nothing good in theatres anymore." Or worse: "I wanted to go, but my husband won't see 'chick flicks.'" This lose/lose mentality destroys the careers of women filmmakers, and is equally damaging to women in the audience.

I can remember when cars were only marketed to men, but now that women make purchasing decisions for themselves and their families, car manufacturers design new models that target the needs and preferences of women. I can remember when the only women in Congress were the widows of powerful congressmen, but now powerful women head committees in the Senate and the House of Representatives. Every time women mobilize to create positive change, the world becomes a better place for our daughters and their daughters' daughters. Do I really believe this? Yes, I do!

One day, after I'd been telling people about the "Celluloid Ceiling" for over four years (in lectures and presentations, online and in print), Martha Richards of WomenArts (aka the Fund for Women Artists) called me and said: "Let's collaborate," and so we did. With energy and passion as our only resources and the internet as our primary tool, Richards and I declared our intention to celebrate the first International SWAN Day on March 29, 2008 and voila! Women celebrated SWAN Day in 2008 at over 160 events in eleven countries on four continents!

Four years later, there have been over 700 International SWAN Day events all around the world including Argentina, Australia, Bosnia-Herzegovina, Bulgaria, Canada, China, Croatia, France, Germany, Ghana, India, Indonesia, Israel, Italy, Jamaica, Kenya, Philippines, Romania, Uruguay, Wales/U.K., and, of course, the USA. Our simple message—Support Women Artists Now—has quantifiable momentum.

I hope this book will convince **you** to make a personal commitment to our SWAN cause: buy theatre tickets; rent DVDs; fill your Amazon and Netflix streaming queues; seek out films by women and help build buzz. Women filmmakers are depending on you, and even though most of them don't realize it yet, women in the audience are counting on you too.

The fifty reviews included in this book barely scratch the surface. When you're done reading it, you can find hundreds of additional reviews of movies by women filmmakers posted on my Blog *The Hot Pink Pen* (www.TheHotPinkPen.com).

If a tree falls in the forest,
but no one is there to hear it,
does it still make a sound?

This isn't just a philosophical question;
it's a question with very real relevance.

Art is a dyadic process:
artists need audiences/audiences need artists.

Support **W**omen **A**rtists **N**ow!

Penny's Picks
is dedicated to my mother, Helene Huttner,
and my mother-in-law, Juanita Miller.

ACKNOWLEDGEMENTS

Deep gratitude to all the wonderful women who have inspired me, challenged me, and held my feet to the fire since 2002.

Special appreciation to summer interns Alma Garcia and Brigid Presecky, and editor Sylvia Franklin, who helped me pull all of this together, as well as Melissa Wilks who designed the cover art and all graphics.

As always, my greatest thanks go to husband Richard and BFF Dorthea: You are my right hand and my left hand, and together you keep me grounded. None of this would be possible without you!

"We started this line of research [about the Celluloid Ceiling] about a decade ago...

There was a lot of press coverage at the time suggesting that women had finally achieved parity with men in the entertainment business, both on-screen and behind-the-scenes, so we just started counting...

My research clearly shows that if you have women working behind-the-scenes on a film (as producers, directors, screenwriters, etc.) you get more female characters on screen. It is a statistically significant and consistent finding over the years...

If you can change women's representation in the media, you will change women's place in the world. I think it's that simple."

-- Professor Martha Lauzen

Women Filmmakers & Women Audiences:

By Working Together We Can Improve Options for Everyone!

Presentation by Jan Lisa Huttner

Director of College & University Relations
AAUW-IL, Inc.

Monmouth College
Monmouth, Illinois
March 25, 2004

My purpose tonight is to persuade all of you to become smart movie consumers. I intend to convince you that the decisions we make as audience members can change the kind of options we have when we go to the movie theater.

I'm talking specifically to the women here tonight, because women have to take the lead on this, but obviously we need all the guys with us too. The idea that guys won't go to see films by women because they're "chick flicks" – where does that come from? It's important for guys to see films by women. In the end, we're all just people, and movies have a lot to teach us all about each other.

When the Oscar nominations were announced in January, recognition for women filmmakers took a tremendous leap forward. My belief is that the future now rests in our hands. Will 2004 be the beginning of a trend toward truly equal opportunity for women filmmakers, or will we look back and say 2004 was a fluke? If 2004 is a fluke, then next year we will simply return to the same dismal statistics that we've had in the past, and the gains we made in 2004 will quickly be forgotten.

I'm going to start with a little historical background about the concept of the "Celluloid Ceiling." I'll define what it means and review the research that supports it. Then I'll tell you why I think we've entered a new "golden age" based on three new technologies that have changed the balance of power, expanding the options for filmmakers and audiences everywhere.

****

Martha Lauzen is a media specialist, a communications professor at San Diego State University in California. She received her Ph.D. from the School of Communications at the University of Maryland, and for the past 11 years she's been tracking women's roles behind-the-scenes in film and in television. Tonight, I'm only going to talk about Professor Lauzen's film research. But you should know that she's done comparable research on opportunities for women behind-the-scenes in television as well.

Professor Lauzen has been compiling statistics for over ten years, and the really scary thing is that things are not only NOT getting any better for women behind-the-scenes in Hollywood, but things are actually getting worse. Her statistics defy the trends in almost every other occupation, where women's participation has been growing over time, albeit gradually. (Just think about how many women are in the U.S. Senate today versus twenty years ago!)

Here's what Professor Lauzen does: every year, she complies a list of the top 250 films released that calendar year (defined by domestic box office grosses).Then she tabulates all the behind-the-scenes roles. She looks at six categories: Producer, Executive Producer, Director, Screenwriter, Editor, and Cinematographer. How many women filled those roles in the top 250 films? There's a cumulative effect here. Her research clearly shows that the more women you have working behind-the-scenes on a film, the more women then come onto that film (especially when women are in either the producer or the director role).

Her last set of statistics was released in June, 2003, based on data collected from all the films released in calendar year 2002. In calendar year 2002, for the top 250 films (measured by domestic box office grosses for that year), men had directed more than 9 out of 10 films on the list. Even worse, 83% of those top 250 films had no female screenwriters. Now, a lot of films have two, sometimes three, or maybe even four credited screenwriters. So the fact that 83% of the top 250 films had no female screenwriters at all is a pretty shocking statistic. Objective, quantitative results like that should wake people up to the fact that something is seriously wrong.

Sure enough, when Professor Lauzen's team did their "content analysis" of these films, they found that 77% of the identifiable protagonists were male, and only 16% were female. One statistic demonstrated that you had a greater chance of being seen on the screen if you were an extraterrestrial than if you were an Asian woman! I hope we all agree that this is not good, right?

> **It means that there are whole categories of people in the world that nobody ever sees on screen, people whose stories are never told. It means that there are very few films depicting the real lives of women and girls around the world today. It also means we have a limited number of films about important female historical figures.**

Here's an example: Did any of you see the film *Pollock* from 2000? It starred Ed Harris as painter Jackson Pollock and Marcia Gay Harden as his wife, artist Lee Krasner. Both leads were nominated for Oscars, and Marcia Gay Harden actually received the Oscar that year for Best Supporting Actress. If you think back, you'll see that was a huge upset. Everybody was expecting Kate Hudson to win for her role as the loveable groupie "Penny Lane" in *Almost Famous* (because she'd won the Golden Globe Award).

When Marcia Gay Harden won her Oscar, I thought: "Great! They can just take *Pollock*, re-cut it, and then add on details about the life of Lee Krasner." Then you would have a new movie called *Krasner* (the sequel to *Pollock* so to speak). Now you need to understand that Jackson Pollock died in his early 40s, but Lee Krasner lived into her 70s. This woman led an amazingly important life, not only as an artist in her own right, but as the manager of Jackson Pollock's estate. She pretty much changed all the rules for marketing American art after he died. She was a very, very influential person in the world of modern art.

When I interviewed Barbara Turner (the woman who wrote the screenplay for *Pollock*), I asked her: "Are we ever going to see *Krasner*?" She looked at me with this big question mark on her face. Then she realized what I meant, and she said: "No, not in this lifetime, Jan." Now I ask you: Why is that? What makes Jackson Pollock's life more important or more inherently interesting than Lee Krasner's life? Why should that be? But as long as the power players in Hollywood believe that audiences won't turn out for films about women, movies like *Krasner* will never be made. Now, you're all thinking: what about *Frida*? Trust me, we'll get there!

****

Women can fight back now because we have three new technologies.

First of all, we have Digital Video (DV), which allows new filmmakers to make movies on the cheap using handheld cameras. Did any of you see the film *Thirteen* by Catherine Hardwicke? She came to Chicago to do a presentation at the Gene Siskel Film Center a couple of weeks ago, and she said there were only two tripod shots in the entire film.

All the other shots in *Thirteen* were done with a handheld camera. She was literally chasing the characters around the set with her camera. It makes the film feel very real. You can actually get into the actor's faces and see into their characters.

Digital Video is great news if you're a new filmmaker with a big vision and a small budget. Catherine Hardwicke said she started making *Thirteen* with the money she got from taking out a second mortgage on her house. She wrote a part for Oscar-winning actress Holly Hunter, and Hunter liked what she saw, so she came aboard as Executive Producer. Hunter brought the project more visibility, more "buzz," and enough money to complete post-production. And in the end, Holly Hunter got an Oscar nomination this year (for her role as the mother in *Thirteen*) because Hardwicke had created a fabulous "meaty" part for her. So Digital Video is important because it's cheaper to make a good film than ever before. If you have the vision and the commitment, you can do it!

The second new technology is the DVD. Because of the DVD revolution, films can find an audience even if they don't get wide theatrical distribution. For example, the movie *Anne B. Real* (directed by Lisa France) just came out on DVD. It played at a lot of film festivals last year, but I think it only opened theatrically in New York and LA, so it could qualify for an Independent Spirit Award. Well, *Anne B. Real* received two Spirit Award nominations last year: Best Feature under $500,000 (the John Cassavetes Award) and Best Debut Performance (for star JaNice Richardson).

It's a wonderful movie, but it won't be included in Professor Lauzen's 2004 statistics because it won't ever make the list of the Top 250 measured by domestic Box

Office grosses. But you can see it now on DVD, and if you like it, you can tell your friends, and they can tell their friends. And the next time you see that a "Lisa France movie" is playing at your favorite theater, maybe you'll go, right?

Word-of-mouth brings us to the third new technology, which is the Internet. You can find specialized websites and ListServs now that are devoted to promoting films by women. A prime example is called "The First Weekenders Group." You can sign up for their list, and every week they will tell you which new movies directed by women are about to open. You can add your own opinions to the content of these websites, and you can even start your own word-of-mouth campaign: you tell your friends and they tell their friends. Because we now have the Internet, we can bypass the big marketing campaigns that are run by the studios, and actually take control.

****

So WE have to get the word out. WE have to generate "buzz." Does this really work? Yes! Here are two success stories from calendar year 2002—movies that definitely generated sufficient box office revenue to make Martha Lauzen's list in 2003.

Frida (I promised I would get to *Frida*) opened to mixed reviews in November, 2002. Nevertheless, women everywhere really loved *Frida* and they told their friends to see it. This wonderful film about a larger-than-life heroine eventually received six Oscar nominations and won 2 Oscars. But director Julie Taymor wasn't nominated for Best Director, and there was a huge outcry from women on the Internet. (I did a whole lot of screaming about this myself ☺)

One year later, in 2004, Sofia Coppola became the first American woman ever nominated for a Best Director Oscar. I don't think this was a coincidence; I think this milestone nomination was really meant for Julie Taymor. But this wasn't the first time in Oscar history that Academy members had to play catch-up.

Our second victory in 2002 was *My Big Fat Greek Wedding*, which now holds the record as the most successful Indie in movie history. The budget for *My Big Fat Greek Wedding* was $5 million and it grossed $240 million in the USA. (This is just the domestic box office revenue, not counting video, DVD, soundtrack, or overseas grosses.) *My Big Fat Greek Wedding* was a "little" movie written by a woman, based on her own experiences. By the night of the Oscars, Nia Vardalos had come out of nowhere to receive a nomination for Best Original Screenplay.

Real women like us were responsible for these two success stories, not mainstream film critics. Take a look at the blurbs in the movie ads in your local paper this Sunday. There are a lot of male film critics in the world! This is a particular bugaboo of mine because I live in the city of Chicago. Chicago is a huge city with a very diverse population, and yet most of our movie choices are controlled by three middle-aged white guys. Now I know Roger Ebert (of the *Chicago Sun-Times*), Jonathan Rosenbaum (of the *Chicago Reader*), and Michael Wilmington (of the *Chicago Tribune*) are very different people, and I don't mean to imply otherwise, but please don't tell me they represent the diversity of opinion in a big city like Chicago.

When Roger Ebert published his 2003 Oscar predictions, he wrote: "Salma Hayek [nominated for Best Actress] has the role of a lifetime in *Frida* but the film got more respect than affection." I read that condescending comment and I just couldn't believe my eyes. *Frida* got six nominations and every woman I know loved it, so who's opinion was this? I know it wasn't my opinion. Was it yours?

Then there's David Denby, film critic for the *New Yorker* magazine. (People think of the *New Yorker* as a "woman-friendly" publication because Pauline Kael used to be their primary film critic. News flash: Pauline Kael was retired for years, and now she's dead!) David Denby wrote a full four-column review of *8 Mile*, including a picture of Eminem, and then at the bottom of these four columns, he tacked on half a column about *Frida*:

> "I have to admit that after an hour or so of this Punch-and-Judy show with its noisy drinking, hurling of brightly painted kitchen items, partings and reconciliations, I was ready to knock both lovers flat with a large red chili pepper. Still given its ramshackle construction and its repetitions *Frida* is much better than it has any right to be."

Wow! Is that what YOU saw when you saw *Frida*? If you had just read reviews and/or looked at the blurbs from the critics without listening to word-of-mouth from your sisters, would you ever have put *Frida* on your personal "Must See" list?

Do you any of you remember the reviews for *My Big Fat Greek Wedding*? They were really horrible. One (male) critic even wrote: "This is a movie that was made for my grandmother." The reviews were really horrible, and yet many women loved this movie. So, OK, it wasn't the greatest movie of all time and artistically I don't think it's in a category with *Frida*, but it was a lot of fun and it told the story of real women's lives in a very funny way. That's good enough for me!

****

So now it's up to us—to the collaborative efforts of women filmmakers and women audience members. We have three new technologies: We have Digital Video as the means of production; we have DVDs as the means of distribution; and we have the Internet as the means of communication.

Always remember that people in backrooms are tabulating what we do. When we choose films by women filmmakers we put our money where our mouths are, and believe me, Hollywood notices. Every time one of these "little" movies succeeds, it increases the probability that more will be made. That's how the system works.

Women have proved themselves to be "smart shoppers" in every other domain, so trust me on this: If we want to smash the "Celluloid Ceiling," we can!

© Jan Lisa Huttner (4/1/04)—full text condensed & edited for posting

The New York Times

June 30, 2002

FEMALE DIRECTORS; Male Critics

To the Editor:

Re "An Impatient Sisterhood" by Dana Kennedy [June 2]:

In seeking explanations for the career frustrations of prominent female directors, why not try looking closer to home?

Who reviews films, on staff, for The New York Times? Three men. Who reviews films for The New Yorker? Two men. When the National Society of Film Critics published its recent book of 100 "essential films," how many of the contributors were women? Four out of 41.

I'm willing to bet that if more major publications hired more female film critics, then more films by women (which, surprise, surprise, are often films about women) would get the kind of critical buzz that leads to box office clout.

JAN LISA HUTTNER

Chicago

The writer is creative director of Films for Two: the Online Guide for Busy Couples (www.films42.com).

International Woman's Day

Presentation by Jan Lisa Huttner

Director of International Relations/AAUW-IL, Inc.

Southern Illinois University
Carbondale, Illinois
March 8, 2007

Ladies of Carbondale: I am so excited to be here today! I'm going to start by telling you a bit of history about the WITASWAN project so that you can share AAUW-Illinois' pride in what we've all created together.

The seed that has sprouted into our AAUW-Illinois WITASWAN project was planted on June 2, 2002. I opened up my Sunday *New York Times* and read an article about women filmmakers and how hard it was for them to make it in Hollywood. Why did that article appear on that particular day? It was the Sunday before *The Divine Secrets of the Ya-Ya Sisterhood* opened nationwide, and the question posed by the reporter (Dana Kennedy) was: Why does it take so long for woman filmmakers to get the green light?

The Divine Secrets of the Ya-Ya Sisterhood was an interesting case in point because director Callie Khouri had received an Oscar in 1992: Best Original Screenplay for *Thelma & Louise*. Normally, the way things work in Hollywood, if a screenwriter writes a screenplay that wins an Oscar, well, that screenwriter is the new "hot thing," and gets plenty of opportunities for future projects. But that assumes, of course, that the screenwriter in question is a guy. If the screenwriter is a woman and she makes a film that really resonates with women all across the world, and she ends up getting an Oscar, even though most of the male film critics ignored her film (or worse), then funny how she winds up getting frozen out for a decade or so.

In her prep for Sunday *New York Times* article, Kennedy interviewed Martha Lauzen, a Communication Professor at San Diego State University in California, who has done statistical analyses of what she calls the "Celluloid Ceiling." We already know about glass ceilings in the business world and marble ceilings in government; the film world equivalent is the "Celluloid Ceiling," and Lauzen has been doing statistical analyses for over 13 years, showing how the situation is actually getting worse. More than 90% of the top 250 films distributed in the United States last year (as measured by domestic box office) were directed by men. That's more than 90%...

Back to June 2, 2002: I read this article in my Sunday *New York Times,* and since I had loved *Thelma & Louise,* I'm very eager to see *Ya-Ya.* I'm intrigued by Kennedy's question: Why is it that women have so much trouble succeeding in the film world? I never expect Kennedy to conclude that women don't really want to be directors because they lack commitment. This is 2002: Are you kidding me?!?

For the first time, I write a letter to *The New York Times*: "Dana Kennedy is very quick to offer the 'blame the victim' explanation... Why not try looking closer to home?" I point out that all three of the film critics at *The New York Times* are men, as are both of the film critics at *The New Yorker.* "I'm willing to bet," I write "that if more major publications hired more women film critics, then more films by women (which, surprise, surprise, are often films about women) would get the kind of critical buzz that leads to box office clout."

A couple of weeks later, I'm in Linda Henning Cohen's car and we're driving south to Bloomington for the AAUW-Illinois Summer Board Meeting. I'm still all energized about this Celluloid Ceiling issue, and Linda (who was the incoming Program Vice President) says: "Maybe you can do a program about this at Spring Convention?" "Okay, Jan," I say to myself, "now you've got a cause and a deadline!"

And when I get back to Chicago on Sunday after the board meeting: guess what? My husband is standing at the door with *The New York Times!!!* My first letter ever to the

Sunday *New York Times* got published—a statistical impossibility!!! And not only did they publish it, but they hired a woman film critic (Manola Darghis) soon after. Maybe that's just a coincidence, but I think they received a message and they heard it.

With my letter in *The New York Times,* I'm unstoppable. I start arranging my program for Spring Convention, and good friend suggests a film called *A Jury of Her Peers.* She connects me with the filmmaker (Sally Heckel), Sally sends me a screener, and I love it. Soon it's May 3, 2003, and I'm with Sally Heckel at the Hilton in Lisle. Forty-four people watched *A Jury of Her Peers* together (a film that had been out of circulation for almost twenty years at that point), and it really resonates. The idea that women have something important to say but men aren't listening—that basic scenario becomes very real for all the people in the room that day.

So the movement now known as WITASWAN really started that day (May 3, 2003) with forty-four people in a hotel room in Lisle, Illinois. Sally Heckel was so moved by our response to her movie. She hadn't seen it with an audience for years, and she was touched by the fact that women were really embracing what she worked so very hard to commit to film.

The first speaking invitation came from Donna Sproston of Monmouth Branch. The next thing I knew I was on my way to Monmouth to show *Jury* and then I came here to SIU-C to show it, and soon I'm going all around the state to campuses and branch meetings north, south, east and west.

The next AAUW-Illinois Summer Board Meeting convened in July 2004 under the leadership of incoming President Kim Benziger, and board members agreed that we should roll-out this new "let's support women filmmakers" project at the five Fall District meetings. I formed a planning committee and we vigorously attacked the question of a project name.

We asked AAUW-Illinois branch members all around the state for input, and we searched Google for potential acronyms. I wanted something with syllables (like UNICEF), but our first attempt WITA (for "Women in the Audience") turned out to be the URL of a right-wing political Web site. So we added a few more letters to get COWITA (for "Coalition of Women in the Audience"), but my best friend, Chicago Branch member Dorthea Juul, said: "Oh no, Jan, we can't be COWITA because then everyone will call us the cows!"

After more brainstorming, we came to WITASWA (for "Women in the Audience Supporting Women Artists"), and we thought: "Well it kind of sounds like an Indian tribe," but the first Fall District Meeting on October 2nd was getting ever closer… We were almost ready to start printing flyers about WITASWA, when committee member Barbara Zeitz was hit by a thunderbolt: "Jan, if we put an N on the end of WITASWA, then we can all be swans!!!"

The answer was right there waiting for us to discover it, and once Barbara gave us "the n," we all knew it was right. We're swans! Who wouldn't want to be a swan, especially in preference to a cow? Right? Of course right!

So now we're "swans" because we **S**upport **W**omen **A**rtists **N**ow.

Women everywhere have voices, visions, dreams; they have things that they want to say, and we have to support women filmmakers so they will have more opportunities to make their films and get their voices heard. This isn't just an issue for Americans; this is an issue for women all around the world.

Clearly it's not just a coincidence that women filmmakers tend to be very interested in women's lives. In general, women filmmakers do not treat their female cast members one way or the other based on their body parts. That's why what we're doing is really important and has so much resonance.

I love that this is an Illinois-based initiative coming from our nation's heartland. To people in New York and LA, I say: "Remember that old showbiz question: 'Will it play in Peoria?' Well let me tell you where Quincy is: Quincy is one step to the south and one step to the west of Peoria, and WITASWAN plays great in Quincy!!!"

© Jan Lisa Huttner (3/8/07)—full text condensed & edited for posting

POINTS SYSTEM

As you read the reviews, you will see that I gravitate to films with a certain heft and weight, films that "stay with me" and "nourish me" on some level after the credits roll. Here are my ratings categories:

✳✳✳✳✳ 5 = A work of art
"The whole is greater than the sum of its parts."

✳✳✳✳ 4 = A fine film
"The whole is equal to the sum of its parts."

✳✳✳ 3 = A good movie
"The whole is less than the sum of its parts."

CHAPTER ONE
Films rated 5

"The whole is **greater** than the sum of its parts."

Fish Tank
Written & Directed by Andrea Arnold

**Principal Actors: Katie Jarvis
with Michael Fassbender & Kierston Wareing**

"Mia" (Katie Jarvis) lives in an East London housing project with her mother "Joanne" (Kierston Wareing) and her younger sister "Tyler" (Rebecca Griffiths). Joanne is an arrested adolescent more comfortable in her frilly pink bedroom than her own kitchen, so Mia and Tyler are both growing up wild. Then a handsome man named "Connor" (Michael Fassbender) enters their family circle. Is he the husband/father they've all been waiting for... or just another predator?

Penny's Points: ✱✱✱✱✱

"Mia" (Katie Jarvis) lives near the marshy edge of the Thames River with her mother "Joanne" (Kierston Wareing) and her younger sister "Tyler" (Rebecca Griffiths). There don't seem to be many adult men around, and there's certainly no evidence of a husband for Joanne or a father (or fathers) for her two daughters. Do these three people even share one common family name? Who knows?

What they do share is a rundown apartment in an East London housing project, large enough for three, but in poor repair.

Crusty dishes are stacked on countertops, but nothing simmers on the stove, and the only nutritious item coming from the fridge is a single container of yoghurt. It would be easy enough to fault Joanne, until we realize how young she is. She's an arrested adolescent more comfortable in her frilly pink bedroom than her own kitchen. Is it any wonder that Mia and Tyler are growing up wild?

Mia's escape comes through dancing. She's found an abandoned apartment where she can be alone, and she spends most of her time practicing hip-hop routines. She dresses in baggy sweats, like a rapper, and throws her ferocious energy into new moves.

One day Mia is at home, mimicking Black dancers on TV, when a barefoot stranger comes up behind her. It seems Joanne has a new boyfriend named "Connor" (Michael Fassbender) who now fancies himself the cock of the walk. How else to explain the fact that Connor swaggers into the kitchen wearing nothing but a low-slung pair of jeans? Mia is startled, but she quickly adjusts. Connor's clearly not the first man to enter their family circle though Joanne's bedroom door.

We think we know where this is going, and unfortunately, both Connor and Joanne behave just as badly as we expect them to, but I can't remember ever meeting a character quite like Mia before. Actress Katie Jarvis fills the frame in every single scene, foul-mouthed but clearly intelligent, damaged and needy, but also resourceful and resilient. This is her first screen role and she's terrific.

Writer/director Andrea Arnold came out of nowhere to win a "Best Live Action Short" Oscar for her 26-minute film *Wasp* in 2005 (about an even younger and even more overwhelmed single mother), and the following year her first full length feature, *Red Road,* won the Jury Prize at Cannes. In 2007, Arnold was named "British Newcomer of the Year" by both

BAFTA (the British Academy of Film and Television Arts) and the London Critics Circle. *Fish Tank* brought Arnold additional honors in 2009 (including one more from Cannes as well as two from my own Chicago International Film Festival).

The most remarkable thing about this stream of accolades is that all three films tell stories from an undeniably female point of view. Yes, British audiences accept female protagonists more readily than their American cousins do. Women novelists like Jane Austen, Charlotte Bronte, and Virginia Woolf have been widely-read and much admired through-out the generations, and new film adaptations of their work keep coming in an unceasing flow.

Andrea Arnold doesn't make "typical" British films. You won't find any carriages or ball gowns, polished manners or polite conversations in Andrea Arnold's world! Her heroines are raw and bruised, always pushing again and again at the edge of acceptable behavior. For all that, though, they never lose our sympathy; no matter what they do, we still worry about them and will them to succeed.

The film opens with Mia searching for her best friend, "Keeley" (Sarah Bayes). When she finally finds her, Keeley is one of a gaggle of girls performing a provocative dance routine for an ogling assortment of neighborhood boys. The more Mia tries to engage her, the more Keeley tarts it up until Mia finally explodes, stomping off enraged and alone.

Then we meet Joanne, and watching Joanne as she dances alone in their flat, we understand. Mia doesn't want to move the way Joanne and Keeley move. Dancing is Mia's way of expressing physical exuberance, and the last thing she wants is to attract male attention.

But Connor is always watching Mia and finding seemingly innocent reasons to touch her in ominous ways. He's so handsome and likeable that we want to believe the best of him. Maybe Connor really is the husband/father they've all been waiting for? Warming to him, Mia lets her guard down, never admitting either to herself or to her mother that Connor makes her uneasy. And so the sexual tension inside the flat builds to an inevitable climax.

However, even though she's only fifteen years old, Mia is totally self-directed, and Connor quickly learns that he can't control her any more than Joanne can. Learning their lessons the hard way, Connor's betrayal becomes something of a wake-up call for the whole family.

Arnold mirrors Mia's coming-of-age with scenes of a physical environment that's also in transition. Will the Thames marshes, so beautifully captured here by cinematographer Robbie Ryan (who also created the forbidding urban landscapes in Arnold's *Red Road* as well as the intensely-lit interior spaces in Sarah Gavron's *Brick Lane)* remain industrial wastelands, or will they one day become wildlife sanctuaries? Arnold sees the potential for both outcomes, good and bad, and Mia's ability to step into the muck and pull treasure from muddy water is cause for hope.

SPOILER ALERT:
Please do NOT read until after you have seen *Fish Tank*

One night, mid-movie, Connor gets Joanne drunk, puts her to bed, and then heads back to the living room to watch TV with Mia. When he finally makes his move (the move we now know, with regret, that he's been planning all along), Connor compares himself to Mia's friend "Billy" (Harry Treadaway). Billy is a **boy,** Connor crows, but I'm a **man.**

Clearly Connor has convinced himself that Mia is having sex with Billy because that makes it easier for him to have his way with her. Yes, yes, Mia's just a kid, she's only 15, but she's already sexually active, so what's the problem?

The problem is we never see Mia having sex with Billy, and what we know of their relationship makes intercourse very unlikely. So is Mia a virgin?

I know it's a very subtle point, but why isn't Mia worried about blood? The sofa is beige. If she's a virgin, then shouldn't Mia be afraid of blood stains? Surely she doesn't want Joanne to know what's just happened on her beige sofa!

Here is what I think: I think Mia is not a virgin when she has sexual intercourse with Connor. I think Connor is just one more man who took advantage of the daughter while "romancing" the mother. So no, Connor is not the first predator to violate Mia, but I do think maybe, just maybe, he will be the last. I think, on some level, Joanne knows why Connor leaves her so abruptly, and she will do a better job protecting Tyler in future. And I think Tyler has been watching too. She's a pretty clever kid, and I think she will protect herself better than Mia did.

But what about Connor? Has Connor learned anything? He's enraged when Mia violates the sanctity of his home and endangers his daughter "Keira" (Sydney Mary Nash), and rightfully so. But the fact that he acts out, hunting Mia down and smacking her around, indicates to me that he's learned nothing. My guess is that Keira will continue to pay for the sins of her father, a father now more likely to be overprotective because he knows only too well what beasts men can be.

In her perceptive article "The year the girls grew up on screen," *Guardian* columnist Barbara Ellen writes: "Far from not wanting your daughters to see [these films], perhaps we should insist on it: give them 'ideas,' make them think a bit."

I agree! Films like *Fish Tank* and *An Education* (which Ellen mentions), and *The Lovely Bones* (which she does not) tell their stories from the girl's point of view, and "the hoariest of all coming-of-age clichés, the wonderful sexual awakening, gets undermined… Indeed, with these feminine teen verité films, it seems there are fewer clichés, period. No one gets to fall in love happily or innocently."

Girls deserve to know the truth about the world; we need to tell them all the things we've already learned the hard way, and make sure they know they're not alone. Many girls have been victims in the past and many girls will be victims in the future, but maybe, just maybe forewarned is forearmed.

Men like Connor and "David" (in *An Education*) might well be handsome and charming, but that doesn't make them any less dangerous, and even a monster like serial killer "George Harvey" (in *The Lovely Bones*) can hide his demons for years before his crimes catch up with him. But maybe, just maybe, seeing their private behavior revealed on screen will make some predators ashamed of their behavior—unforgivable behavior that has no excuse and is not sanctioned by society.

Fish Tank ends with one last dance. This time Mia leads from the middle, with Joanne to her right and sister Tyler to her left, and they're all dancing Mia's way, for themselves and for each other. The path ahead will not be easy; the deck is stacked against them and they all know it. But their last dance together, while bittersweet, is touched with grace. One lives in hope!

© **Jan Lisa Huttner (2/15/10)—Special for WomenArts**

Frozen River
Written & Directed by Courtney Hunt

Principal Actors: Melissa Leo
with Misty Upham & Charlie McDermott

Two women, one white (Melissa Leo) and one Native American (Misty Upham), form an unlikely bond in perilous circumstances, smuggling illegal immigrants across the frozen St. Lawrence River in the dead of winter. Filmmaker Courtney Hunt's first feature won the Grand Jury Prize at the 2008 Sundance Film Festival. The Hot Pink Pen agrees: Frozen River *is one of the best films released this year.*

Penny's Points: ✵✵✵✵✵

Midway through filmmaker Courtney Hunt's powerful first feature *Frozen River,* two women make a fateful decision. They barely know one another and each woman has a lifetime of good reasons for suspicion. If they fail, the consequences will be enormous for all concerned, but success will do nothing to improve the material circumstances of either woman's family.

The most remarkable thing about the way Hunt films this scene is that it's totally visual. "Ray Eddy" (Melissa Leo) and "Lila Littlewolf" (Misty Upham) both know what they have to do, they do it, and they move on. When I try to imagine two men in similar circumstances, I can't picture the scene without dialogue. What they're planning to do is totally crazy. Surely one would try to bully the other into changing his mind?

But for as verbal as most women are most of the time (and we are!), sometimes a situation is so clear that no words are required. Furthermore, once they've shared this experience, Ray and Lila find they've bonded, and their new relationship propels the film to an unexpected but well-earned conclusion.

Ray is married to an addict, and they have two sons. One is a teenager and one is still a kid, and the age difference between her two boys dramatizes how long Ray has been struggling to keep her marriage going. Her job is their only regular source of income, but the guy she works for is a sneering 20something who's pushing her to quit. Dealing with customers, cops, and others with power over her is physically painful; every time she forces herself to smile, her self-esteem takes another blow. Whatever tenderness she still has is saved for her boys. If she's someplace they can't see her, her haggard face reveals that bitterness and exhaustion have pushed her to the edge.

Lila lives alone on a Mohawk Reservation straddling the St. Lawrence River. One part of the reservation is in New York and the other part is in Quebec. Mounties patrol the Canadian side and state troopers patrol the American side, but as long as she's on the reservation, Lila is under the jurisdiction of the Tribal Council. Friends repeatedly warn her that smuggling is too risky, but Lila won't stop, even though she already has a record as a juvenile offender. She needs money and she doesn't believe she has legitimate ways of earning any.

No one in *Frozen River* gets a detailed back story. Almost everything is told in the present tense, and most of what Ray and Lila reveal about themselves comes through body language. But when I spoke with Leo, she said Hunt was very precise and always knew just what she was after: "The script was extraordinarily complete." Asked what most interested her most about Ray, Leo said: "It's easy to do things you know are right, but more interesting to see someone do something against her better judgment."

Frozen River is a perfect film. Every character is carefully drawn and totally believable, and I was immediately engrossed in the story line. The ending took me completely by surprise, all the more so because I'd seen the trailer multiple times and thought the plot would be more conventional. Hunt clearly delights in teasing us, luring us into the theatre with chase scenes and gun play so that she can tell us a finely-crafted story about two women otherwise invisible in today's multiplex.

If I ruled the world, then Melissa Leo would have received Best Supporting Actress nominations in 2004 (playing "Marianne" in *21 Grams)* and in 2006 (playing "Rachel" in *The Three Burials of Melquiades Estrada).* If she's not nominated for Best Actress this year (for "Ray"), I'll be howling in protest!

© **Jan Lisa Huttner (7/31/08)—Special for WomenArts**

King Kong
Directed by Peter Jackson
Adaptation by Jackson
with Fran Walsh and Philippa Boyens
(Based on original 1933 screenplay by Ruth Rose)

Principal Actors: Naomi Watts
with Jack Black & Adrien Brody

With eighty more years of film technique at their command (screenwriting, screen acting, etc, as well as special effects), Jackson & his team have transformed a mythopoetic Depression Era classic into not only the best film of 2005, but one of the greatest films ever made.

Penny's Points: ✳✳✳✳✳

When you're a professional film critic, you see tons of movies. This may sound like fun, but think about it: I've seen lots of really bad and "just OK" movies in the past year. At a certain point, watching becomes purely physical; my body literally tells me if I'm engaged or bored. So when I see a new film that absolutely takes my breath away, I want everyone to know.

I'll admit that my expectations were relatively low when I went to see Peter Jackson's new remake of *King Kong*. I'd seen the original *King Kong* as a kid, and while I certainly enjoyed it, I never became a *King Kong* fanatic. I found the theatrical versions of Jackson's *The Lord of the Rings* trilogy tedious, long on battle scenes and short on character development. (I much prefer the extended DVD versions of *The Fellowship of the Ring, The Twin Towers,* and *The Return of the King.*)

But the new *King Kong* completely overwhelmed me. The drama held me captive for three full hours. It felt far shorter than several 90-minute turkeys I could name, and I left the theater on a high.

Most of the people fascinated by the original *King Kong* focus on its revolutionary "stop-motion" animation and visual design. As a tie-in to the release of the new *King Kong*, Warner Video has just released a new two-disc "Collector's Edition" of the original, with a wonderful documentary on the second disc called *RKO Production 601: The Making of Kong, Eighth Wonder of the World.* But here's a curious fact: barely, in passing, do any of the "talking heads" even bother to mention that the person who actually wrote the original screenplay was a woman!

Merian C. Cooper, the man most responsible for the original *King Kong*, was a WWI hero who formed a partnership with fellow veteran and Hollywood filmmaker Ernest Schoedsack in the early 1920s. Together Cooper and Schoedsack made several popular documentary adventure films in exotic places like Iran and Thailand. By the time Cooper began planning *King Kong*, Schoedsack was married to Ruth Rose, a writer who had accompanied Cooper and Schoedsack on many of their trips.

Cooper hired famous British author Edgar Wallace to write a screenplay but he died unexpectedly, so his treatment was passed along to screenwriter James Creelman. When the script still fell short, Cooper made an appeal to Rose, even though she'd never written a screenplay before. "Give it the spirit of a real Cooper-Schoedsack expedition," he told her, and when she was done, he said: "I don't think another human being in the world could have given me the simple direct fairy tale dialogue that she did. It was just what I wanted."

Skip ahead seventy years, and the remake also shows the woman's touch. In addition to Jackson, the new *King Kong's* authors are Fran Walsh (Jackson's wife) and Philippa Boyens (their longtime writing partner). I'll let you guess who probably wrote the brontosaurus stampede scenes and who probably wrote the more intimate scenes between heroine "Ann Darrow" (Naomi Watts) and her two primary co-stars. In a recent interview, Boyens said she and Walsh were always delving into character motivation as they worked: "We found the key moments in the storytelling… We literally watched hours and hours of gorilla footage. Then you understand that gorillas do communicate. They do have a language."

In other words, men may argue about the intelligence of non-verbal animals, but women, who are used to nurturing babies and pets, know there are other ways to "speak." So while the men in *King Kong* are primarily interested in forcing a powerful "beast" into submission, Ann admires his strength and sees both his pride and his vulnerability.

Despite what some reviewers have told you, I don't think Ann and Kong ever "fall in love." Ann's in love with "Jack Driscoll" (played by Adrien Brody), who makes a heroic transformation of his own in the course the film. What Ann and Kong share is empathic understanding; they look into each other's eyes and see the souls within. Cooper was always clear about his goal. "I'll have women crying over Kong before I'm through," he said, and believe me, I cried plenty.

Final words: *King Kong (2005)* is a film that you really should see on the big screen, so you can surrender yourself to the richness of its images and sound design, and also participate fully in the audience experience. Just remember: bring your tissues!

The Life & Times of Hank Greenberg
Documentary by Aviva Kempner

Key Participants: Hank Greenberg
& His Jewish Fans

Greenberg played for the Detroit Tigers in the '30s, joined the Army pre-Pearl Harbor, then returned to baseball in 1945, hitting innumerable homeruns every year in defiance of his era's Nazi stereotypes. In this ebullient biodoc, Greenberg's forever preserved as a Jewish hero as well as a great American dreamer.

Penny's Points: ✹✹✹✹✹

The Life & Times of Hank Greenberg is a joyously linear documentary which traces the career of "the baseball Moses" from the Bronx who became one of America's greatest Jewish sports stars. This ebullient film, which combines a tight focus on its central character with a concise evocation of the context in which his life resonated, captured 10 Film Critics Association Awards in 2001 (including the critics associations in Chicago, Florida and New York).

"Hammering Hank," who began his Major League career with the Detroit Tigers in 1933, was a national hero throughout the 1930's. He reached his peak in 1938, the year he came within two homeruns of breaking Babe Ruth's record of sixty homers in a single season. (Ruth's record held until Yankee Roger Maris finally smashed it in 1961.) Greenberg made a different kind of headline in May of 1941 when he became the first star ballplayer to enlist in the military. After four years of service, he astonished everyone by returning to the Tigers in June 1945 and hitting a homer in his very first game.

Although not a religious man, Greenberg was conscious of his heroic status, especially among young Jewish boys, and he made a deliberate decision to attend Yom Kippur services in 1934 even though the Tigers were in middle of a pennant race. He was devoted to his family, but remained a bachelor for many years. When he finally married in 1946, he married heiress Coral Gimbel. (The Gimbels, prominent Jewish philanthropists, owned a department store empire that included Saks Fifth Avenue.)

Throughout his career, he dealt with anti-Semitic taunting from the bleachers. During the 1935 World Series in Chicago, the umpire had to intervene to stop catcalling from the Cubs bench. He never exploded, but never forgot. Years later, when Jackie Robinson broke the color barrier in 1947, Hank was the first opposing-team player to offer encouragement.

Director Akiva Kempner draws from a huge archive of stills and filmed interviews, including hours of interviews Hank taped before his death in 1986. The brisk 95 minute run time is filled with testimonials from fellow players and sports writers, personal reminiscences from family members, and golden memories from Jewish celebrities such as actor Walter Matthau, lawyer Alan Dershowitz, and Senator Carl Levin.

Spicing up this visual feast is a fabulous soundtrack which opens with NPR's Yiddish Radio Project host Henry Sapoznick singing "Take Me Out to the Ballgame" in mameloshen. Mandy Patinkin reprises the number during the closing credits. Stuffed in between is a full banquet of musical treasures with particular emphasis on classic swing numbers such as Benny Goodman's "Sing, Sing, Sing."

© **Jan Lisa Huttner (4/1/05)—Special for World Jewish Digest**

Look Both Ways
Written & Directed by Sarah Watt

Principal Actors: Justine Clark
with Anthony Hayes & William McInnes

Australian drama Look Both Ways *is a downunder version of American Oscar-winner* Crash, *but its polar opposite in every way--subtle where* Crash *is bombastic, true to the little moments of real people's lives where* Crash *manufactures big moments of melodramatic overstatement. Yes, disease and death are the elements around which writer/director Sarah Watt builds her narrative, but something magical happens in the telling: instead of doom and gloom, Watt somehow creates one of the most life-affirming films of the year.*

Penny's Points: ✸✸✸✸✸

In the opening moments of the terrific new Australian film *Look Both Ways,* an artist named Meryl (Justine Clark) witnesses a train accident. Meryl is already in a dark mood. Two weeks earlier her father died suddenly with no advance warning, and heading home from her mother's house, where she's been since his funeral, Meryl's mind is filled with dreadful images. When the police question her, she must struggle to focus. She knows she did not imagine the accident. She saw a man playing with his dog, and that man is now dead.

Two journalists arrive, a reporter named "Andy" (Anthony Hayes) and a photographer named "Nick" (William McInnes). Although they've never met before, Nick is Meryl's neighbor, so they leave the scene together, each of them pretending to engage in normal conversation despite the tragedy that's brought them together. But like Meryl, Nick is primarily absorbed in a personal shock of his own; he's recently been diagnosed with testicular cancer.

These are the elements, death and disease, around which writer/director Sarah Watt builds her narrative. But something magical happens in the telling: instead of doom and gloom, Watt somehow creates one of the most life-affirming films of the year.

Look Both Ways is a downunder version of *Crash,* and its polar opposite in every way, subtle where *Crash* is bombastic, true to the little moments of real people's lives where *Crash* manufactures big moments of melodramatic overstatement. The characters in *Crash* are enraged by their circumstances. The characters in *Look Both Ways* understand that, as residents of the "first world," their personal catastrophes are simply the stuff of life. There are only two options: draw comfort from your connection with those around you or live in lonely misery.

Like her heroine, Watt studied art but failed to make a living as a painter. Meryl takes the practical step of working for a greeting card company. Watt turned to animation. Her breakthrough came with the 1995 animated short *Small Treasures* which won the OCIC Award at the Melbourne International Film Festival (given to "the most outstanding Australian film [of the year] promoting human values"), and went on to win the "Baby Lion" for Best Short Film at that year's Venice Film Festival. Clocking in at 15 minutes, *Small Treasures* is the story of "Jane" (voiced by Rachel Griffiths) who is pregnant with her first child. Like Meryl, Jane sees danger everywhere, but she still embraces life with all its inherent tragedy. Jane is clearly Meryl's precursor.

One of the most welcome features of *Look Both Ways* is its sexual balance. In addition to Meryl, Nick, and Andy, there are three more primary characters, "Anna" (Lisa Flanagan), who is Andy's pregnant girlfriend, the widow of the man killed in the accident (Daniella Farinacci), and the man who was driving the train at the time of the accident (Andreas Sobik). These six individuals are surrounded by a rich ensemble of colleagues, family members, and friends, comprising a cross-section of Adelaide (located near the center of Australia's southern coastline) but representing small "first world" cities everywhere.

(In contrast Los Angeles, as depicted in *Crash,* is a male-dominated world with relatively few women. Furthermore, while the male characters in *Crash* have 3-dimensional lives, the women in *Crash* are primarily defined by their roles in the lives of the male characters. None of the female characters in *Crash* has a backstory.)

Andy and Anna are the most verbal characters in *Look Both Ways,* and as they make their big decisions (keep the baby? stay together?), they have the most amount of dialogue. Meryl and Nick are both more visually than verbally-oriented, and that's the first thing they come to appreciate about each other. The morning after the accident, Nick, out for an early run, rescues one of Meryl's rejected watercolors from her trash bin at almost the same moment Meryl is scrutinizing Nick's photograph of the accident scene (which dominates page one of her local newspaper).

Meryl's vivid inner life is depicted in fluid animated sequences. She doesn't just imagine disasters. A trip to a local swimming pool with her girlfriend finds her gliding past reefs and brilliantly-colored tropical fish with her mind's eye. Nick, on the other hand, runs through huge stacks of still photographs in his mind. They provide background on his extensive travels as well as insight into the systematic research he does when he learns about his condition. These staccato collages also add an element of suspense. Does Nick have the capacity to connect dots?

The widow and the driver have no dialogue. Their two stories are presented in separate arcs; as the other characters resume their daily lives, hushed scenes of the widow and the driver add punctuation marks of grief, reconciliation, and hope. All six lives have been forever changed by the accidental death of a man hit by a train. The widow and the driver must face each other before either can begin to heal.

The obvious message of *Look Both Ways* is that there are no easy answers for any of us. There is no way to make our parents, friends, or family members immortal. There is no way to keep our children safe. There is no way to protect ourselves from death's inevitability. Whether the end of one specific life is caused by disease, accident, or whatever, at some point, every life will end.

In itself, this is trite, of course, but Watt's message comes at a critical time. Westerners in general, and Americans in particular, have been so traumatized by terrorism since 9/11, that we've willingly traded precious civil liberties in the attempt to make our world safer. Watt insists that we face the truth. The more we attempt to protect ourselves, the more we cripple ourselves, making the life we actually have less worth living. It's a difficult message to fully absorb, but it's the message that we most need to hear right now.

© **Jan Lisa Huttner (3/31/06) —Special for WomenArts**

Trouble the Water
Documentary by
Tia Lessin & Carl Deal
(Based on footage filmed by Kimberly Rivers Roberts)

Key Participants:
Kimberly Rivers Roberts & Scott Roberts

Award-winning documentary about Hurricane Katrina melds first person and third person perspectives into a taut 96 minutes that both captures the moment and provides the context. Aspiring rap artist Kimberly Rivers Roberts just happened to have a new camcorder with her as storm clouds started building over New Orleans, and that helped her to become "a witness to history," making real to us lives we all held so cheaply before the catastrophe shamed the nation. A triumph of documentary filmmaking, sure to be a contender as '09 Oscar buzz builds.

Penny's Points: ✱✱✱✱✱

Once upon a time I studied cognitive psychology, and sometimes I still find myself flashing back to graduate school days. Specifically I've seen a lot of documentaries recently that bring to mind "the Hawthorne effect." You may not be familiar with this term, but you're certainly familiar with the idea. Here's how it's defined on the Harvard Business School website: "…the phenomenon in which subjects in behavioral studies change their performance in response to being observed…" For example, I really enjoyed *Surfwise* (a stranger-than-fiction story about a Jewish doctor who raised a brood of kids in a trailer, convinced that they would learn more on a beach than in a classroom), but the big family reconciliation scene at the end left me screaming "Hawthorne Effect!"

However, the outstanding new doc *Trouble the Water* sent my mind in the opposite direction, all the way back to Shakespeare: "Some are born great; some achieve greatness, and some have greatness thrust upon them." Back off, Shakespeare scholars: I know these words are used to mock the Malvolio character in

Twelfth Night, but sometimes they actually fit, and this is one of those cases.

Trouble the Water is the story of an aspiring rap artist named Kimberly Rivers Roberts who just happened to buy herself a cheap camcorder one day. According to the press kit, her intentions were totally mundane ("recording birthday parties and family moments"), although I suspect she had hopes of learning to use it professionally as well. But whatever she was thinking the day she bought it, the fact is that Kim had her camcorder at the ready just as storm clouds started building over New Orleans on August 28, 2005, and having the power to capture images of her reality helped turn Kim into Superwoman. In other words, the subject (namely Kim) changed her performance in response to the fact that she was suddenly an observer.

Sitting comfortably in our theatre seats, we're watching real lives in jeopardy. Even as she kept filming, Kim knew her survival was in doubt, and she was unsure if she would live long enough to save her footage. But Kim not only survived Hurricane Katrina, she became a source of inspiration and hope to everyone around her.

Once the immediate crisis was over, post-Katrina chaos sapped the strength of most mortals, but Kim was relentless. She kept telling people about her treasure, and she kept filming, even as she and her husband Scott transported their small group of dependents to relative safety at a rural homestead.

Meanwhile filmmakers Tia Lessin and Carl Deal had gone down to New Orleans with preconceived plans that were quickly abandoned. Tia had been one of the producers of *Bowling for Columbine* and *Fahrenheit 9/11* (two of Michael Moore's most financially and critically successful films), and Carl had managed all the archival footage on both films. Tia had also been one of the producers of *The Awful Truth,* Moore's Emmy-nominated

TV series. They weren't looking for Kim, but when they met her they quickly recognized her as a working-class hero in the raw, and they knew they had the funding connections to go the distance.

The finished product is a triumph of documentary filmmaking. It melds first-person and third-person perspectives into a taut 96 minutes that both captures the moment and provides the context. Critics and audiences are all applauding. *Trouble the Water* won the Grand Jury Prize at the 2008 Sundance Film Festival as well as three awards at North Carolina's "Full Frame Documentary Film Festival" (the Full Frame/Working Films Award, the Jury Award, and The Kathleen Bryan Edwards Award for Human Rights). With its 96% Fresh score on Rotten Tomatoes.com, *Trouble the Water* is sure to be a contender as Oscar buzz builds.

For sure Kim has earned her "15 minutes of fame," and my hope is that she uses it to keep holding our nation's feet to the fire. Ironically, Hurricane Katrina may well be the best thing that ever happened to Kim, but that's only because we now know her as "a witness to history," someone with the courage and stamina to speak out for all those whose lives were held so cheaply, not only during the catastrophe, but before it and after it as well.

© **Jan Lisa Huttner (9/2/08)—Special for WomenArts**

CHAPTER TWO
Films rated 4.5

13 Conversations About One Thing
Directed by Jill Sprecher
Screenplay by sisters Jill & Karen Sprecher

Principal Actors: Clea DuVall
with Alan Arkin & Matthew McConaughey

Four sets of characters act out their own Manhattan mini-dramas and yet mysterious threads connect the four separate stories, creating a highly satisfying whole. Alan Arkin plays a divorced, middle-aged businessman named Gene. Gene is worn-out and cynical. His son is in jail and his company is facing cutbacks. The guys on his staff expect Gene to protect them, until it becomes clear to them that Gene himself isn't always in the senior management loop. Clea DuVall plays Beatrice, a young woman who works for a high-end cleaning service. Beatrice is earnest and hard-working. She survived a childhood accident and considers every new day a gift from God, but her co-worker thinks she's a patsy.

Matthew McConaughey plays Troy, a handsome young prosecutor who's a rising star in the DA's office. Born with a silver spoon in his mouth, Troy has never known any way but "up." When life throws him a curve, he suddenly realizes that he's never developed any coping mechanisms. John Turturro plays Walker, a Mathematics professor at Columbia University who believes in discipline, order, and reason. But one day he's mugged, and the feeling of violation completely unnerves him. These four principals are all searching for happiness – but happiness proves to be as elusive and ephemeral as a rainbow.

Penny's Points: ✹✹✹✹½

13 Conversations has a great deal in common with films such as *Amores Perros*, *Pulp Fiction*, *Run Lola Run*, and *Short Cuts*, all of which play with overlapping timelines, and questions of chance, fate, and destiny. When you find yourself "in the wrong place at the wrong time," do you ask yourself: "How did I get here?" Do you wonder what you did wrong, or what one thing you might have done differently? If so, this is the film for you.

Each one of the four principals comes to regret a specific moment in time that, once done, cannot be undone. The poignancy of these lost moments is heart-breaking precisely because, in each case, the decision made in that moment is so completely in character.

Unlike the other films I listed above, however, *13 Conversations*, is hushed and muted, and most of the violence is implicit. Alex Wurman's melancholy piano-driven soundtrack sets the contemplative mood. The acting is first rate across the board; Arkin's performance as Gene is truly outstanding.

If you prefer straight narrative lines, this film will drive you crazy. But if you believe the world is mostly gray, with rare instances of pure white or black, then I predict that this film will really intrigue you.

This is the Sprecher sisters' second feature film. (The first was *Clockwatchers,* starring Toni Collette, Lisa Kudrow, and Parker Posey.) The Sprechers obviously have a talent for casting, finding perfect vehicles for their beautifully drawn characters.

© **Jan Lisa Huttner (6/20/02)—Special for DVDWolf**

An Education
Directed by Lone Scherfig
Screenplay by Nick Hornby
(Based on a memoir by Lynn Barber)

Principal Actors: Carey Mulligan
with Peter Sarsgaard & Olivia Williams

Lone Scherfig's terrific new film An Education *opens in a classroom in an English suburb in the early 60s. A con artist named David (Peter Sarsgaard) seduces an impressionable teenager named Jenny (Carey Mulligan), but after a few semesters in his "University of Life," Jenny returns to her teacher, Miss Stubbs (Olivia Williams), and Miss Stubbs is the one who provides the final boost required to launch Jenny from her time into our own.*

Penny's Points: ✳✳✳✳½

Lone Scherfig's terrific new film *An Education* opens in a classroom. The place and time are very specific: we're in an English suburb in the early 60s. Born right after World War II, these teenage schoolgirls have all grown up with post-Blitz austerity. They don't know what we know—if they can just hang on, The Beatles, Twiggy, Carnaby Street, and "Swinging London" are all right around the corner. But in the meantime, the most liberated role model on offer is Jane Eyre, a heroine created by novelist Charlotte Brontë over one hundred years before scene one.

Jane Eyre is, in fact, the subject under discussion when we first meet "Jenny" (Carey Mulligan) and her severely bespectacled teacher "Miss Stubbs" (Olivia Williams). Then the school day ends, and Jenny's "Mr. Rochester" arrives in the guise of a handsome man named "David" (Peter Sarsgaard). Like someone sent from Central Casting, David appears to be both cultured and financially prosperous, and he quickly charms Jenny's parents, "Marjorie" (Cara Seymour) and "Jack" (Alfred Molina). They're not concerned that David is considerably older than Jenny, after all, wasn't Mr. Rochester at least twice Jane's age? In fact, only one person seems resistant to this budding romance: Miss Stubbs.

But how can Miss Stubbs, with her Cambridge degree, compete against David, a self-described graduate of "the University of Life"? Jenny, always a superior student, dives head first into his new curriculum: concerts and restaurants, jazz clubs and race tracks. David's seemingly inexhaustible resources even include the perfect set of travel companions, his suave business partner "Danny" (Dominic Cooper) and Danny's gorgeous girlfriend "Helen" (Rosamund Pike).

Like all teenage girls, Jenny thinks she understands sexual exchanges. How often has she already paid for one movie ticket with one good night kiss? Jenny knows David is spending a lot of money on her, and she's decided she's ready to pay the price. But an air of foreboding hangs over *An Education*. Has everyone forgotten that Mr. Rochester locked his first wife up in an attic? Oh, Jenny!

An Education is loosely based on a brief memoir by Lynn Barber, a highly accomplished and very well-known English journalist. But Scherfig and screenwriter Nick Hornby (who wrote the autobiographical charmer *Fever Pitch* as well as box office hits *About A Boy* and *High Fidelity*) wisely jettison the memoir's bitterness and implicit self-loathing, and focus forward. Jenny is who she is on screen, and she has no idea who she will become (even if we think we do). "The actor should never play the ending," Scherfig told me, "and in a way, with this film, the ending is after the film is finished."

An Education sets out the full range of female options available to a girl like Jenny, with teachers like Miss Stubbs and the Headmistress (Emma Thompson) on one end, and mother Marjorie and neighbor "Sarah" (Sally Hawkins) on the other, while glamorous Helen twinkles at her from the wrong side of respectability. Jenny sees all these possible futures and intuitively rejects them, but breaking free of cultural expectations is no easy task for someone raised to be "a good girl."

When I spoke with Scherfig, I referred to *An Education* as an ensemble piece (by which I meant all the individual characters were extremely well-delineated), but she quickly corrected me: "No, it's Jenny's film—you're supposed to see things with her eyes!" But then Scherfig acknowledged: "If it didn't have all the layers, then the film would not be 'epic' as opposed to 'dramatic'... It's almost **the time**, and not Jenny, that's the main character in *An Education*."

Carey Mulligan is lovely as Jenny. She's smart and pretty and carries the center with a quick tongue, expressive eyes, and graceful body language. I'm not sure if she can bear the hype of being labeled "a new Audrey Hepburn," but I love that she's being compared to one of Hollywood's most bankable leading ladies, and I hope screenwriters write more parts for her.

Peter Sarsgaard adds another complex role to his already fine resume. David must be so smooth and charming that Jenny's parents not only admit this predator into their home, but are also willing to accept him as a permanent part of their lives. If I ruled the world, Sarsgaard would already have at least one Oscar on his shelf (for his supporting role in *Kinsey*) as well as additional nominations for his performances in *The Dying Gaul* and *Shattered Glass*. Perhaps playing David will finally bring him the multiplex attention he deserves, but this role isn't really much of a stretch for him.

The great surprise is Olivia Williams as Miss Stubbs, her depth of character used to counterbalance Sarsgaard's dazzling surface. Best-known as Bruce Willis' wife in *The Sixth Sense,* Williams, like Sarsgaard, has a long list of well-regarded supporting roles, but made dowdy here, this very beautiful woman really touched my heart. Miss Stubbs is a formidable presence; although both her look and her affect are constrained, she clearly has a discerning eye, acute intelligence, and a well-developed conscience (a quality otherwise in short supply).

Looking at *An Education* as an epic (like *Ben-Hur*) explains a great deal. A mature man seduces a young girl—this drama is a cultural staple with a curious hold on the female imagination (as evidenced by the continued popularity of *Jane Eyre* and all her literary and cinematic progeny). But the fact that we're finally learning to question it as "a romance" can be attributed to the fact that writers like Lynn Barber are finally telling the story honestly from a real girl's point of view.

But here's the problem: the multiplex is not a woman-friendly place, and films with female protagonists are hard to sell (all the more so when they're made by woman filmmakers). So expect the marketing campaign for *An Education* to use glamorous photos of Jenny and David, augmented by clips of Jenny with her father Jack, to lure audiences into the theater, burying Miss Stubbs in the background along with Marjorie, Helen, etc, etc.

Don't be fooled! In this film, a teacher literally saves the day. After a few semesters in "the University of Life," Jenny returns to her teacher, and Miss Stubbs is the one who provides the final boost required to launch Jenny from her time into our own.

SPOILER ALERT!!!
Please do NOT read until AFTER you have seen
An Education

As a Jewish-American critic, I am often perplexed about the representation of Jews in popular culture. I sometimes watch films about characters I know are Jewish, but they're not identified as Jews, and they're played by actors seemingly selected to throw audiences off track. Adapting *The Devil Wears*

Prada for the screen, for example, Jewish writer Aline Brosh McKenna removed Jewish identifiers from her two lead characters, "Andy" (Anne Hathaway) and "Miranda" (Meryl Streep), both of whom are clearly identified as Jews in Lauren Weisburger's source novel. When I asked her why, McKenna said: "We were trying to streamline the book and we had a lot of stuff to deal with, and it didn't seem like that [the fact that both characters were Jewish] was a part of it."

So what to make of the fact that David is explicitly identified as Jewish in *An Education?* In Lynn Barber's memoir, her Mr. Rochester isn't just Jewish, he's actually lived in Israel and may even be Israeli. (Lynn keeps trying to locate his accent but never quite succeeds.) He tells stories about his kibbutz days, and when he calls Lynn years after the end of their relationship, he calls her from Jerusalem.

These details are completely deleted from the screenplay, and what little remains of David's Jewish background has its primary pay-off in Jenny's second scene with her school's Headmistress: "He's a Jew? You're aware, I take it, that the Jews killed our Lord?"

From a Feminist perspective this is a real mistake, because in their third and final scene together, the Headmistress nails it. Jenny says: "I suppose you think I'm a ruined woman," and the Headmistress replies: "You're not a woman." The regal Emma Thompson is making a critical plot point here: a girl does not become a woman just because she's had a sexual relationship with a man.

I hate to see the tremendous power of these words diminished because they come from the mouth of someone already discredited as an anti-Semitic bully. Furthermore, the historical facts add an extra level of anxiety for Jewish viewers: the film is set in 1962 and the villain is a Jewish man in his late thirties. So where was David before, during, and immediately after WWII?

And here past and present collide: Sony Pictures Classics is opening *An Education* in American theaters in October '09; meanwhile, in Switzerland, Roman Polanski (a Jewish man known to have "a taste" for young girls) awaits extradition for crimes committed in 1977. Many of Hollywood's alpha males are howling in protest, but most of Hollywood's alpha females, such as they are, remain mute. And as a Jewish Feminist, I sit here in Chicago appalled that some people actually add the Holocaust to the list of excuses for Polanski's execrable behavior.

The Jenny we meet in *An Education* is telling her story in the present tense. She's in a state of adolescent bewilderment. She does things she knows she shouldn't do, sometimes playing out the fantasies of her school chums, sometimes just to thumb her nose at her oblivious parents. I'm not just condemning sex acts here; under David's tutelage, Jenny learns to lie, cheat, and steal.

Here's how Lynn Barber concludes her memoir: "I learned to not trust people... So that when, thirty years later, I heard that 'Minn!' on the phone from Jerusalem, I hated him more, not less, for all the intervening years."

It will take "our Jenny" several decades to find these words, so it's up to us to supply the disgust over what occurs in the here and now. We must look beneath the pretty surface of the romance, and demand to see what David keeps hidden in his attic. David is a con man. He had young girls before Jenny, and he will have young girls after her. If the real David cherished memories of the real Jenny in later years, it's probably because she's one of the few who managed to get away from him before he got tired of her and moved on.

There is no Miss Stubbs in Lynn Barber's memoir; she has nothing good to say about any of the adults who were responsible for keeping her safe. If we fail Jenny now, we've earned the same low grade.

The Beaver
Directed by Jodie Foster
Original Screenplay by Kyle Killen

Principal Actors: Mel Gibson
with Jennifer Lawrence & Anton Yelchin

"Walter Black" (Mel Gibson) is stuck at the bottom of an all-consuming depressive cycle, and his wife "Meredith" (Jodie Foster) has lost hope. Then Walter discovers a ratty old hand puppet, and a miracle occurs: Walter is able to reclaim his voice through "the beaver." Beaver's ebullient personality lifts Walter from the depths and starts him on a manic rise, and one by one, everyone falls under Beaver's spell. Director Jodie Foster keeps her Oscar-winning actor self on a tight leash, but her intelligence grounds the film and helps everyone else in it to shine. Major Depression is a serious and widespread illness, so forget everything you think you know about Mel Gibson (the man), and just watch The Beaver *for the promise of light at the end of a very dark tunnel.*

Penny's Points: ✳✳✳✳½

When we first see "Walter Black" (Mel Gibson), he appears to be a prosperous middle-aged guy floating in the beautiful pool behind his deluxe suburban home. But the first close-up on his face instantly reveals that Walter's life is actually a nightmare; he's deeply mentally ill and stuck at the bottom of an all-consuming depressive cycle.

Walter's wife "Meredith" (Jodie Foster) is exhausted, their teenage son "Porter" (Anton Yelchin) is enraged, and their young son "Henry" (Riley Thomas Stewart) is filled with inchoate sadness. Everyone has lost hope, and thinking she must sacrifice her marriage in order to save her sons, Meredith finally asks Walter to move out.

With no energy left to protest, Walter packs up and drives away. Then he discovers a ratty old puppet, and putting his hand inside the plush torso brings back sense memories of happier times. Suddenly a miracle occurs: instead of seeing himself playing "Beaver" while cavorting with his kids, Walter finds himself conversing with Beaver directly.

Beaver's ebullient personality completely takes over, lifting Walter from the depths and starting him on a manic rise. One by one, everyone falls under Beaver's spell: first Henry, of course, then Meredith, then the people in Walter's company, then the "liberal media" (Matt Lauer, Jon Stewart, and Terry Gross of National Public Radio all have cameo roles), and finally even Porter.

And watching them together, the actors on the screen and the people in the audience fuse as we begin to participate in the story too. Rationally, we all know that Beaver can't exist without Walter. Since Walter isn't a trained ventriloquist, his lips are always moving whenever Beaver "speaks," and Walter makes no attempt to hide himself (like a Muppet puppeteer) while Beaver entertains the crowd. And yet, emotionally, we all understand that Beaver is also more than Walter, just as all artistic creations come to take on a life of their own beyond their creators' conscious intent.

The dynamic between artist and muse, who paints and who poses, who writes and who reads, is underlined by the subplot in which Porter is drawn into a soulful romance with "Norah" (Jennifer Lawrence), a person more adept than Walter at hiding her secret despair. As the valedictorian of their high school class, Norah must give a speech at graduation, so she hires Porter to write it for her. Porter's empathy for Norah, fed by his adolescent longing, opens his heart, and even though his ferocious goal is to be his father's opposite in every way, Porter too begins to speak his own truest thoughts through the voice of another.

Director Jodie Foster keeps her Oscar-winning actor self on a tight leash. We never get to know much about Meredith beyond her roles as wife and mother, and it seems the director only cast the star in this film so she could be an active maternal presence both in front of the camera as well as behind it. Foster's intelligence grounds the film and helps everyone else in it to shine.

The choice of Mel Gibson for Walter was particularly inspired and watching them together is like watching a high-flying trapeze act at the center of a three ring circus. With Foster physically there to return to after every emotional flip and turn with Beaver, Gibson gives the most heartfelt performance of his tumultuous career.

Director Foster asserts herself in the film's very first moments by showing Gibson as Walter literally flagellating himself on screen. I felt like she was speaking directly to me: "Yes, I know; you're bringing all your mixed feelings about *The Passion of the Christ*, Opus Dei, Catholicism and anti-Semitism into this theatre with you, Jan, but push them all out of your mind right now and watch my movie!"

Yes, ma'am! When I left the screening room approximately two hours later, I realized I'd completely forgotten about Mel Gibson (the man/the persona). I only cared about Walter and Norah, and artists everywhere struggling so hard to tell compelling personal stories that capture, with awe, our shared humanity.

I'm certain Foster worked very hard to make Norah a fully realized character, and Lawrence's performance burnishes the Oscar nomination she received last year for *Winter's Bone*. Beautiful young actresses are often badly misused these days, but together Foster and Lawrence make Norah a strong and significant part of a drama that could easily have devolved into a more routine father/son story. Without Norah's solid presence,

Porter's transformation would strain credulity, but Lawrence's performance sets a high bar and gives Anton Yelchin room to grow. To become the man who will be worthy of Norah means, of course, that Porter must find a way to meet his father halfway.

Major Depression is a serious and widespread illness. Since it's all "in the head;" no one can see it or touch it; the main symptoms (fatigue, irritability, feelings of isolation, etc.) are insidious, hovering at the edge of awareness, easy to ignore, excuse or deny. In our culture, which embraces "men of action" ("the strong, silent type"), Major Depression is especially traumatic for adult males, and the consequences can be devastating for a man's family and everyone else in his orbit.

So bravo to Foster and her entire cast and crew, their eyes all fixed on the potential for light at the end of a very dark tunnel.

SPOILER ALERT!!!
Please do NOT read until AFTER you have seen *The Beaver*

I predict that reactions to *The Beaver* will depend in large part on how specific individuals understand the history of Walter Black's relationship with the beaver puppet. Therefore I decided to go back and test my own "theory of origin" before posting this review, and now, having seen *The Beaver* a second time, I can tell you for sure that a case can be made either way.

Here's what I saw: After Meredith asks him to move out, Walter drives to a liquor store and buys way too much booze. When he opens the trunk of his car to stash it, we can clearly see that the trunk is already filled with boxes, but except for an old tennis racquet, none of the contents are visible. Walter removes the box with the tennis racquet and drops it into the dumpster. That's when Walter sees—and we see—the beaver puppet for the first time.

Question: Where did the beaver puppet come from? Did Beaver come from the trunk of Walter's car (in the box with the tennis racquet), or was Beaver already in the dumpster before Walter came out of the liquor store?

My Answer: Beaver came from the trunk of Walter's car. When Walter sees Beaver in the dumpster, he's seeing an old friend from playtimes past, and when Walter starts talking in Beaver's voice, he's using a voice created long ago for conversations with his kids. So this is not a new voice; this is a voice Walter has had in his head for years.

In most instances, we either see Beaver from behind (with Walter in close-up), or Beaver and Walter sharing one frame. In both cases, Walter's lips are always moving. Foster never uses any special effects to imply that Beaver's voice comes directly from the puppet, nor does Walter ever show any special skill as a ventriloquist. So even Walter knows that Beaver's voice is his own, and that's how he introduces Beaver with his "this person is under the care of a prescription puppet" card.

By the time Meredith first sees Beaver, Walter and Henry are already at play. We don't see how Henry first reacted when Walter and Beaver came to pick him up at school, so we don't know if Beaver was ever Henry's toy. But the puppet is pretty ratty, so my guess is that Beaver was originally Porter's toy. Regardless, Henry is positively thrilled to welcome both Walter AND Beaver into his life, and that's why Meredith decides to go along with it ... at least for a while ...

Obviously, when I wrote the original draft of my review, I wrote from the belief that Beaver came from Walter's trunk. So I always knew who/what Beaver was, and I had no difficultly suspending disbelief from beginning to end. But as I said above, a case can be made either way, so if you think otherwise, I'm not about to tell you that you're wrong.

Blue Crush

Directed by John Stockwell
Screenplay by Stockwell & Lizzy Weiss

Principal Actors: Kate Bosworth
with Matthew Davis & Michelle Rodriguez

Anne Marie, Eden and Lena live to surf. They share a small house on Oahu and work as housekeepers in one of the local luxury hotels so that they can finance their passion. It takes all their combined resources, and they're barely making ends meet. As the film opens, Anne Marie is on edge. Based on her amateur ranking, she's one of the first women invited to participate in the macho North Shore Pipeline competition. She knows it's a make-or-break event for her. If she does well, she may be recruited by one of the professional teams. So she's training as hard as she can, but flashbacks of a prior wipe-out drain her confidence. One day at work she goes over the edge and she's fired. Eden and Lena want to walk out with her, but she convinces them to stay. They all know how much they need the money, so Anne Marie is suddenly left alone while her buddies go back to the daily grind. With time on her hands and bad memories on her mind, Anne Marie is ripe for trouble. Enter Matt, the hotel guest who just happens to be a handsome quarterback.

Penny's Points: ✳✳✳✳½

Anne Marie, Eden and Lena live to surf. They share a small house on Oahu and work as housekeepers in one of the local luxury hotels so that they can finance their passion. It takes all their combined resources, and they're barely making ends meet.

As the film opens, Anne Marie is on edge. Based on her amateur ranking, she's one of the first women invited to participate in the macho North Shore Pipeline competition. She knows it's a make-or-break event for her. If she does well, she may be recruited by one of the professional teams. So she's training as hard as she can, but flashbacks of a prior wipe-out drain her confidence.

One day at work she goes over the edge and she's fired. Eden and Lena want to walk out with her, but she convinces them to stay. They all know how much they need the money, so Anne Marie is suddenly left alone while her buddies go back to the daily grind. With time on her hands and bad memories on her mind, Anne Marie is ripe for trouble. Enter Matt, the hotel guest who just happens to be a handsome quarterback.

Blue Crush is based on an article by Susan Orlean called "The Maui Surfer Girls" which was originally published in the Fall 1998 issue of *Outside* Magazine. You can read it for yourself in Orlean's recent collection *The Bullfighter Checks Her Make-Up*. In 2001, Orlean was asked to deliver the Johnston Lecture for the University of Oregon's School of Journalism and Communication. The title of her lecture was "Finding the Extraordinary in the Ordinary: Writing about Everyday Life." Asked "What is it about so-called ordinary people that attracts you as a writer?," she replied as follows: "Writing about 'ordinary' people is about following my own curiosity. After doing celebrity journalism, I realized I was more interested in the things I walked past every day, the stuff people usually miss. I'm primarily interested in the tiny master -- a person with a tiny domain over which they are the master. I wrote a piece about a New York City cabdriver who is also the king of the Ashanti tribe in America. After that experience, I realized -- you never know. Any other cab driver I meet, any ordinary person, could be a king. It made me step lightly."

This quote tells me more about *Blue Crush* than anything I've read in the dozens of reviews I've read since the film opened. "Anne Marie" (Kate Bosworth) is, indeed, a tiny master – someone who is very good at what she does, someone who is most alive when she's doing the thing she loves, and someone who spends her days cleaning other people's #$&% (literally) so that she can prove herself on the Pipeline.

It falls to screenwriter Lizzy Weiss and director/screenwriter John Stockwell to place Anne Marie in a coherent, engaging setting. They take the frame from Orlean. Anne Marie lives in a Hawaiian paradise lush with natural beauty, where the economy is almost totally dependent on tourism. Our 50th state resembles a third world country: adult women have lots of children, low wage jobs, and almost no adult male support. No wonder a talented girl like Anne Marie wants to live on the waves as long as she can. Orlean puts it this way: "I spent a lot of time trying to picture where these girls might be in ten years… Maybe these girls are still young enough and in love enough with their lives that they have no special foreboding about their futures, no uneasy presentiment that the kind of life they are leading now might eventually have to end."

For dramatic purposes, Stockwell and Weiss have made their surfer girls a little older. They are on the cusp. Whenever Anne Marie slacks off, "Eden" (Michelle Rodriguez) is there to remind her about what's at stake. They also create a "love object" (Matthew David) to give the film some romantic zing, and add complexity to their heroine's choices. To keep it light, they've made the arc of the plot conform to a typical sports story: great expectations followed by fear of failure followed by triumph.

Personally, I have nothing against genre movies, but I think their success depends on all the little details that flesh out the shell's more predictable elements. In this case, with Orlean's acute eyes and ears to guide them as well as Brian Grazer's powerful muscle to smooth their way, the filmmakers have created a winner. (Grazer is an Oscar-winning producer, an avid surfer, and the father of a 13 year old daughter.) In a summer in which accomplished actresses like Jennifer Jason Leigh *(Road to Perdition),* Frances McDormand *(City by the Sea),* Frances

O'Connor *(Windtalkers)* and Franka Potente *(The Bourne Identity)* were all given "play-doh" parts, Stockwell and Weiss even took the time to create a genuine backstory for their hunk. (Listen for how Matt explains his ability to put a special spin on a football). Do I believe the ending? Let's put it this way. Like millions of people around the world, I watched the Olympics on February 21, 2002. We were all expecting to see Michelle Kwan finally win her gold medal for figure skating, but what we all saw instead was Sara Hughes on the ride of her life. So, yes, I'm a believer!

Blue Crush has everything: an interesting story about a little-known subculture, exciting visuals, and a propulsive soundtrack. What's more, the story it tells is both timely and important. The film opened on August 18, 2002. On September 5, 2002, *The New England Journal of Medicine* released a major study demonstrating precipitous decline in physical activity for adolescent girls between ages 10 and 16. Girls need more images of healthy, strong female bodies. They need more stories in which girls compete against the elements and prevail over their inner demons. And we all need more films in which creative artists like Susan Orlean and Lizzy Weiss are encouraged to express uniquely female points of view. Any film that can sell an important message with both energy and empathy gets kudos from me!

© **Jan Lisa Huttner (9/28/02)—Special for DVDWolf**

Bright Star
Written & Directed by Jane Campion
(Based on Andrew Motion's biography of Keats)

Principal Actors: Abbie Cornish
with Kerry Fox & Ben Whishaw

Bright Star *is the story of a woman named Fanny Brawne who falls deeply and hopelessly in love with a frail young poet. After he's dead, this man becomes the famous John Keats, but when she first meets him, John is a lonely, solitary fellow with sad eyes and thin shoulders. Young girls long for this romantic enthrall; grandmothers reminisce about it tenderly, and in* Bright Star, *Fanny's mother and sister live vicariously through every moment of exaltation and despair.*

Penny's Points: ✳✳✳✳½

The first time I saw *Bright Star,* I left the Chicago Screening Room thinking: "I can't wait to see this film again!" That's a good news/bad news message. The good news is that I really loved *Bright Star,* and I knew I would appreciate it even more after I'd done some homework. The bad news is that if you go in cold, you might leave cold too.

So I'm going to do something I almost never do, I'm going to give away the ending:

John Keats dies of tuberculosis at the age of 25.

If *Bright Star* were a biographical film ("a BioPic") about English poet John Keats, then giving away the ending would either be old news or absolutely unforgiveable. But *Bright Star* isn't really about John Keats (1795-1821) at all; it's about his muse, his "bright star" Fanny Brawne, and John's imminent death is a constant in her life from the very beginning of their brief relationship.

When "Fanny" (Abbie Cornish) first meets "John" (Ben Whishaw), he's a lonely, solitary fellow with sad eyes and thin shoulders. He has almost no money and his family connections are limited, but he has good friends who suspect a talent he's only just finding for himself. One friend, "Charles Brown" (Paul Schneider), offers him shelter in his own home (Wentworth Place), and John soon becomes acquainted with Brown's neighbors, the Brawne family.

Fanny's mother, Mrs. Brawne, is a widow with three children, first Frances ("Fanny"), then Samuel, then Margaret ("Toots"). Her small estate is encumbered by her late husband's debts, and she has raised Fanny to be as sensible and independent as the times will allow.

But soon after meeting, Fanny and John realize they are soul mates, and a doomed two year romance begins. Mrs. Brawne and Mr. Brown both try to intervene, but it's already too late. John watched his beloved younger brother Tom die of tuberculosis, so he recognizes his own susceptibility. Fanny knows the symptoms too; she lost her father to the same disease. Why persist?

Early in their relationship, John teaches Fanny the secret of poetry: we don't dive into a pond so as to reach the shore; we swim to enjoy the water. Just so, John's death is a given, and Jane Campion's film is all about sensuous immersion.

The pace is slow, the language is formal, and 19th Century social conventions require these lovers to sublimate their physical desires. But they achieve consummation through poetry, with words now affirmed to be among the most beautiful ever written in the English language.

The closest cinematic parallel is *Shakespeare in Love,* in which William Shakespeare's muse is "Viola De Lesseps"—a character created by screenwriters Marc Norman and Tom Stoppard to meet the needs of a love story told from Will Shakespeare's point-of view. Jane Campion, on the other hand, doesn't need to fabricate any characters. She knows Fanny Brawne's voice from the letters she wrote to John's sister after his death.

We know Fanny wrote letters to John as well; she saved all the letters he sent her, and his letters reference hers. But where are these letters now? Painter "Joseph Severn" (Samuel Barnett) cared for John during the last months of his life, and he told everyone that John's dying wish was to have Fanny's letters buried with him in his casket. So we must take Severn's word for this historical outcome; we will never know for sure if John deliberately or inadvertently acted to silence her.

When I spoke with Jane Campion, she told me: "Things for me work best when they're both literal and metaphoric—they're part of the story, but they carry more meaning than their literal weight." The literal destruction of Fanny's letters isn't a story Campion can tell in *Bright Star,* but I can tell this story, with all its implicit metaphoric content.

Campion herself luxuriates in the ardent letters John wrote to Fanny. The middle of the film is almost entirely devoted to quotes from actual letters John penned from the Isle of Wight. The first one is dated July 3, 1819.

> My Dearest Lady…
>
> Ask yourself my love whether you are not very cruel to have so entrammelled me, so destroyed my freedom... I almost wish we were butterflies and liv'd but three summer days—three such days with you I could fill with more delight than fifty common years could ever contain…
>
> Be as kind as the distance will permit to your
> J. Keats

Keats goes to the Isle of Wight; Keats goes to Winchester Cathedral; Keats is out and about in London. Meanwhile, Fanny wanders the heaths surrounding Wentworth Place, waiting feverishly for letters which she devours hungrily and then reads over and over and over again. And yet, here is John, in voiceover, complaining about his "entrammelled freedom."

Perhaps there are some women who don't know the agony of "passive" waiting, but I can easily picture my younger self in just such a state. Girls long for this romantic enthrall; grandmothers reminisce about it tenderly. For Fanny, it's all new. Who can possibly understand her? But Campion shows two people living vicariously through every moment of exaltation and despair—her mother "Mrs. Brawne" (Kerry Fox) and her sister "Toots" (Edie Martin). Campion's brilliant invocation of the butterflies in John's letter is *Bright Star's* most purely cinematic sequence.

As Campion told me at the end of our conversation: "What I love about this story is that they were that innocent and pure, and feeling love for each other and getting close and being connected, and then melding their identities into the Keats/Fanny identity, which is where they lost themselves. All psychotherapeutic advice would be 'keep your own identity, and then merge and separate and merge and separate.' Well, they didn't."

No, they didn't, and after I saw *Bright Star* the second time, all I could think was: "Better to have loved and lost than never to have loved at all!"

© **Jan Lisa Huttner (9/29/09)—Special for WomenArts**

Cadillac Records
Written & Directed by Darnell Martin

Principal Actors: Adrien Brody & Jeffrey Wright
with Beyoncé Knowles

Cadillac Records *is a musical history of Chicago Blues starring Adrien Brody as Leonard Chess, Jeffrey Wright as Muddy Waters and a host of other wonderful actors in key supporting roles. Ironically, it didn't get much buzz when it opened on December 5, and it quickly disappeared from theaters when it failed to receive any major Golden Globe nominations on December 11, but luckily it's now available to all on DVD. Tremendously entertaining,* Cadillac Records *has powerful resonance; it was one of my favorite films of 2008.*

Penny's Points: ✳✳✳✳½

Cadillac Records is a history of Chicago Blues, starring Adrien Brody as "Leonard Chess" and Jeffrey Wright as "Muddy Waters." Since musical biopics combine two of my favorite movie genres, I've seen all the likely candidates you can name, from *The Glenn Miller Story* (1954), *Lady Sings the Blues* (1972), and *What's Love Got to Do with It* (1993), to *Ray* (2004), *Walk the Line* (2005), and *Dreamgirls* (2006). Think of similar films before, after, or in between, and I've likely seen them, too. Telling a credible story in approximately two hours while still doing justice to great music is always a challenge. So while I enjoyed all of these films, none of them fully satisfied me. But *Cadillac Records* won me over completely!

The narrative arc of *Cadillac Records* begins in 1941 with the introduction of its two protagonists. McKinley Morganfield was born in Rolling Fork, Mississippi in 1913; Lejzor Czyz was born in Motal, Poland (now Belarus) in 1917. By the time they meet in Chicago in 1947, Morganfield has created the persona of Bluesman "Muddy Waters" and Czyz has reinvented himself as entrepreneur "Leonard Chess," but they both know where they've come from, and they're both determined never to fall back.

Writer/director Darnell Martin lays down key events in each life, one after another, creating the parallel rails which kept them on track for 22 years. While never denying their differences, her primary goal is to illuminate what they had in common. Driving south through miles of open fields on their first road trip together, Muddy asks: "How come you didn't stay your ass in Poland?" And Leonard answers: "How come you didn't stay your ass in Mississippi?" Muddy just laughs.

Leonard has chutzpah, Muddy has talent, and together they agree to gamble big on post-War prosperity. "This is America," Leonard insists early on. "Stop with 'enough.' The word is 'more.'" The Holocaust, never mentioned but always present in the background, has united most Jewish-Americans with African-Americans in the battle against Jim Crow. As simplistic as this may sound now, you won't truly appreciate what you see onscreen if you ignore this common frame of reference.

Most of the film takes place, as it should, right in the recording studio. The Chess Records label (established in 1950) makes its first serious money promoting Muddy's music to Blacks, but Leonard and Muddy soon bring others into the fold. "Little Walter" (Columbus Short) plays a mean harmonica. "Howlin' Wolf" (Eamonn Walker) has a guttural roar. Then "Chuck Berry" (Mos Def) adds a country twang, and suddenly white audiences are dancing to his "Rock & Roll." Leonard surrounds "Etta James" (Beyoncé Knowles) with strings, and she crosses over, too. The times may be a-changin', but that doesn't stop "Willie Dixon" (Cedric Kyles, aka Cedric the Entertainer) from writing more hit songs.

Leonard is a workaholic and Muddy is a womanizer, yet they both find good, patient wives who tolerate their excesses. They have lots of children but no divorces—on screen or in life. By the time Leonard dies (in 1969), their partnership has acquired a mythic dimension. Over the closing credits, Martin tells us that they were both inducted into The Rock & Roll Hall of Fame in 1987 (one year after it opened).

The casting is impeccable. This is the most multidimensional, fully adult performance of Adrien Brody's career (way better than the monotonous misery of his Oscar-winning turn in *The Pianist*). Beyoncé Knowles and Columbus Short both create indelible characters desperately clinging to their music—lifeboats rocked by emotional storms of inner anguish. Mos Def provides just the right cockeyed charisma for Chuck Berry, and Eamonn Walker (a personal favorite of mine since his days as "Kareem Said" on the HBO series *Oz*) burns up the screen as Wolf. Gabrielle Union is sexy, warm, and totally believable as Muddy's wife "Geneva" (particularly in her scenes with Columbus Short), and Emmanuelle Chriqui manages to convey the off-screen evolution of "Revetta Chess", even though she's only seen in snippets. Jeffrey Wright's singing may lack sufficient power in itself, but the music is so strong that it carries him through, and it's hard to imagine anyone doing a better job of embodying Muddy in the dramatic scenes.

Voice-over narration typically annoys me, but in this case there's a perfect fit. Determined to cover the whole Chess/Waters marriage from courtship through "death do us part," Martin gives Willie Dixon the strategic role of "traffic cop"—individuating the members of her huge cast while also providing historical context. (Emmet Till, Rosa Parks, Elvis Presley, and Mick Jagger all make brief appearances, as do recording industry giants such as Alan Lomax and Alan Freed.)

Although he began his career as a songwriter, Willie Dixon ended his life as an impresario, arranging worldwide tours for Muddy and other American Blues giants (just as *Cadillac Records* shows) and helping them access their copyrights and royalties. In 1993, Willie's widow Marie purchased the building at 2120 South Michigan Avenue that housed Chess Records for all the years depicted in the film. She donated it to the "Willie Dixon

Blues Heaven Foundation," and it's now a protected Chicago landmark operating under Willie's motto: "The Blues are the roots; the rest are the fruits." So Martin's decision to use Kyles' booming off-screen voice in this way is both historically accurate and cinematically sound.

Cadillac Records didn't get much buzz when it opened on December 5, and by December 12 most theaters were already pushing films on the Golden Globe list (almost all of which were of much lower quality). *Cadillac Records* only received one Golden Globe nomination (in the Best Original Song category), and it was totally shut out when Oscar nominations were announced on January 22. According to The Internet Movie Database, it grossed a paltry $8.1 million at American box offices and quickly disappeared from view.

What a historical irony! On November 4, 2008, exactly one month before *Cadillac Records* opened in urban theaters, Barack Obama became President-elect of the United States. People all around the world watched as Obama gave his acceptance speech that night in Grant Park (less than two miles from 2120 South Michigan Avenue!), and one of his first official acts, a mere two days later, was to name Rahm Emanuel his White House Chief of Staff. What better moment to open this lively film about Chicago's first triumphant African-American/Jewish-American collaboration? But alas, as I learned way back in college: "The owl of Minerva only flies at dusk."

Luckily, *Cadillac Records* is now available to all on DVD. I've watched it three times already (once with the English subtitles on so I could catch all the dialogue), and I find it gets better and better every time I watch it. Most of the musical numbers (artfully glued together by Terence Blanchard's subtle background score) still send shivers up and down my spine, and the more I look, the more I see the nuanced character development and carefully crafted period detail.

Shout out to Darnell Martin: You Go, Girl! Now when ya' makin' that Bessie Smith biopic starring Queen Latifah?!?

Jan's Final Thoughts

I never read my colleagues' reviews until after I've seen a film for myself, but sometimes I read some of their reviews later, and my mouth falls open: did they see the same film I saw??? In our defense, professional film critics see lots and lots of movies, and often we only have a chance to view something once before turning in our copy. Furthermore, we usually watch films at preview screenings arranged just for us (so we can publish our reviews right before a film opens); therefore most of our editors can't do any fact-checking. No wonder "s--t happens" sometimes!

In this specific case, I missed the critics screening, so I saw *Cadillac Records* for the first time in a regular theater on December 5. Since I was already late, I decided to wait and watch it a couple of times on DVD before writing my review. I even watched it once with the English subtitles turned on so I could catch every bit of dialogue. Maybe I wouldn't have gone to such great lengths if I hadn't been so baffled by some of the things I read. Of course, we're all entitled to our own opinions, and I'd never contest the ratings of colleagues who gave *Cadillac Records* three stars, two stars, or none. But having said that, I still think some of my colleagues saw things in *Cadillac Records* that weren't really there, but they didn't see some obvious things that were…

SPOILER ALERT!!!
Please do NOT read until AFTER you have seen *Cadillac Records*

To my colleagues baffled by a dichotomy ("Darnell Martin can't decide if Leonard Chess was a man who genuinely loved Blues music or someone who merely exploited Blues artists for his own financial gain."), the answer is yes: yes, Leonard Chess genuinely loved Blues music (and the artists who created it), and yes, Leonard Chess made a great deal of money from the music he created with these artists.

Can anyone watch *Cadillac Records* and not see that Leonard Chess literally worked himself into an early grave? His mind is always on business; he's forever "cooking the books" and struggling to keep people productive in spite of their damaged lives and self-destructive habits.

The period right after WWII was an extremely paternalistic era, so, of course Leonard Chess carried all the cultural baggage of his time. But almost all of the Chess Records artists outlived him (by decades!), and I think fair-minded people will understand that he deserves some credit for this fact. Minimally, Darnell Martin wants you to see Leonard Chess the way Muddy Waters saw him, and if you don't, then you won't really understand what Muddy and Wolf are fighting about when the time comes to pay for Little Walter's funeral.

So, OK Jan, let's say Leonard Chess really did "love" Blues artists; was that love literal or metaphorical? To my colleagues who come out of *Cadillac Records* convinced that Darnell Martin thinks Leonard Chess and Etta James had an affair, I say: watch again.

The Leonard Chess we see in *Cadillac Records* is consumed by his need to make money. This is where Martin's references to Poland and poverty become critical. He equates money with power at the most primal level: power to provide, rescue, and yes, "repair the world." Darnell Martin shows Muddy Waters bringing Geneva Wade to orgasm, and she shows Leonard and Revetta Chess in a moment of marital coitus, so if she had wanted to show Leonard Chess and Etta James having sex she surely would have done so.

What *Cadillac Records* tells me is that great music was created through the elemental relationship Muddy Waters had with Little Walter—and that Leonard Chess had a parallel relationship with Etta James. There are no easy labels for these intense collaborations. We've known they had an "erotic" component since Plato wrote his *Symposium,* but what drives them is never the alignment of body parts.

The Leonard Chess we see in *Cadillac Records* knows this; while he's certainly drawn to the flame, we never see him singe his wings. But Beyoncé Knowles singing the Etta James classic *At Last* over and over again while Barack and Michelle Obama dance their way through a night of Inaugural Balls… well now, I think this is just the kind of consummation the Leonard Chess of *Cadillac Records* truly craved!

© **Jan Lisa Huttner (3/21/09)—Special for WomenArts**

Conviction
Directed by Tony Goldwyn
Screenplay by Pamela Gray
(Based on the life of Betty Anne Waters)

Principal Actors: Hilary Swank
with Minnie Driver & Sam Rockwell

After a difficult childhood spent in and out of foster care, "Betty Anne Waters" (Hilary Swank) marries young and starts building a little nest. But when her volatile older brother "Kenny" (Sam Rockwell) is arrested, Betty Anne's world slowly turns inside out. Much to her own surprise, Betty Anne learns she's not the kind of woman who can just walk away, and thus begins a twenty-year odyssey that starts with education (she's a high school dropout!) and ends with passing the Bar Exam so she can become Kenny's attorney of record. Conviction *belongs to its actresses. Major parts, minor parts, bit parts, walk-on parts, no matter—the female talent on display in this film is extraordinary. Beneath the legal drama (with its DNA evidence, motions and appeals) lies the story of a woman who transcends her circumstances, remaking herself into a 21st century heroine of epic proportions.*

Penny's Points: ✱✱✱✱½

After a difficult childhood in and out of foster care, "Betty Anne Waters" (played by Bailee Madison as a child and two-time Oscar-winner Hilary Swank as an adult) just wants to live a normal life. So when she meets Mr. Right, Betty Anne marries young and builds a little nest, lavishing attention on her newborn son. Then her volatile older brother "Kenny" (played by Tobias Campbell as a child and Sam Rockwell as an adult) is arrested, and slowly but surely, Betty Anne's world turns inside out.

At first she's not too worried. Even knowing Kenny's been in trouble all his life, Betty Anne is certain he could never commit murder, so she's sure there's no real evidence against him. But "Nancy Taylor" (Melissa Leo), the arresting officer, is relentless, and Kenny's weak public defender (Marty Bufalini), already overmatched by the zealous prosecutor (Talia Balsam), simply has no good cards in his hand. So Act One of Tony Goldwyn's new film *Conviction* ends with Kenny in jail. Sure it's unfair, says Betty Anne's sympathetic husband "Rick" (Loren Dean), but there's nothing more to be done.

Much to her own surprise, however, Betty Anne learns she's not the kind of woman who can just walk away, and she becomes obsessed with proving Kenny's innocence. In the beginning, her only asset is determination, but as the years pass, she completes a G.E.D., then a community college certificate, then a college degree. By the end of Act Two, about a dozen years after the trial, Betty Anne Waters has passed the Bar Exam, become Kenny's attorney of record, and enlisted the aid of "Barry Scheck" (Peter Gallagher), co-founder and director of *The Innocence Project*, in her appeal process.

So far, everything I've said above is a matter of historical record, but *Conviction* isn't a documentary, *Conviction* is a narrative feature. Yes, these characters (all defined as characters by placing quote marks around their names the first time I introduce them) are based on real people, but real life isn't neatly divided into "acts" played by actors. As a narrative feature, the goal of a film like *Conviction* is to use the tools and techniques of cinema to go beyond fact in order to elucidate the human condition. This it does brilliantly, making *Conviction* one of the very best films I've seen so far in 2010. (I'm a film critic, so in round numbers that means "Top Ten" in a field of at least 200 candidates.)

My first set of kudos goes to Pamela Gray for her eloquent screenplay. Gray creates a feisty young "Betty Anne Waters" character (age 8 or so) and then moves her through decades of increasingly intense life experience. Clever, resourceful, and loyal as a kid, Gray's Betty Anne has no idea how smart she is and no acquaintance with her own inner tigress. Gray makes Betty Anne's professional growth as a lawyer fully believable, all the while showing how the power of her personality drew people to her and kept them on her side through inevitable ups and downs over twenty years.

My next set of kudos goes to director Tony Goldwyn for his excellent casting. The female talent on display in this film is extraordinary. Major parts, minor parts, bit parts, walk-on parts, no matter—in each case, Goldwyn somehow found just the right actress for each role. Since I'm someone who fixates on and remembers female performances, I can tell you he culled from a diverse universe of multiplex, Indie, TV, and stage actresses, each one of whom brings depth and resonance to her own unique corner of Betty Anne's world.

None of Goldwyn's actors falter either. Loren Dean as husband "Rick" is a protective macho presence. Sons "Richard" (Conor Donovan) and "Ben" (Owen Campbell) fill Betty Anne's life with warm sibling banter. Peter Gallagher endows his "Barry Scheck" with compassion and dignity. And Sam Rockwell gives the best performance of his career as "Kenny." If Rockwell isn't nominated for a Best Supporting Oscar in January, then there really is no justice for Kenny Waters in this world.

As a filmmaking team, I also give Goldwyn and Gray kudos for understanding there are no villains in their story. Absolutely every character has a legitimate point of view. In fact, part of Rockwell's accomplishment is to make Kenny so mercurial that we can't really fault "Nancy Taylor" (the arresting officer so poignantly played by Melissa Leo) for thinking he must be guilty even when Betty Anne's evidence shows otherwise.

The last set of kudos belongs to five actresses in ascending order, beginning with Kenny's ex-girlfriends "Brenda Marsh" (Clea DuVall) and "Roseanna Perry" (Juliet Lewis), first seen when they take the stand to testify against him in Act One. Beyond their Act Three contributions to the unfolding legal drama, Brenda and Roseanna are there to remind us who Betty Anne's peers were before Kenny's incarceration sent her down a different path. Since this story is set in New England, I'll invoke Robert Frost here: "Two roads diverged in a yellow wood..."

The person Betty Anne meets on the road "less traveled" is "Abra Rice" (Minnie Driver) a law school classmate who surfaces midway through Act Two and becomes a driving force in Act Three. Driver is so quick-witted and funny as Abra that audience members (especially male audience members) may not fully appreciate her multiple contributions to the narrative. The Betty Anne of Act One has no room in her life for "comic relief," and the Betty Anne of Act Two has no time in her already hectic schedule for a BFF ("Best Friends Forever"). But by Act Three, Abra has become a critical part of Betty Anne's personal and professional life.

Then there's Kenny's daughter "Mandy Marsh" (Ari Graynor). Mandy appears late in the film, well into Act Three, but Graynor's performance packs a totally unexpected emotional wallop. Betty Anne searches for Mandy because she needs something from her mother Brenda, but once they've made a connection, it's Mandy who shows audiences the degree to which Betty Anne has transcended her childhood circumstances and transformed herself into a role model for young women of a new generation. Although Graynor has had several well-regarded supporting roles in other films, "Mandy" is a break-out role for her and she stole my heart.

My final kudos go to *Conviction's* star: Hilary Swank. The actress playing Betty Anne Waters must embody this heroine's magnanimous spirit, of course, but it also helps that Swank already has two Best Actress Oscars on her shelf. With nothing more to prove to anyone but herself, Swank melts into the role, anchoring all the other performances with quiet confidence. And I think she, most of all, appreciates the irony here: in what may well be a Hollywood first, the real person is actually prettier, softer, and more feminine than the actress who plays her!

A few closing words from my October 8th telephone conversation with screenwriter Pamela Gray.

Jan: So Betty Anne's network—being a mother, being a sister, being an aunt, being a friend—these relationships pulled Betty Anne through?

Pamela: Absolutely, absolutely. And I believe that's just one difference between movies where the woman is the heroine [versus a male hero]. Often the male hero is the solo person, moving through [the film] without that community. But I do think the heroine's journey is different in that way. I see that in a lot of movies that are female-driven: they've got community; they're not working in isolation.

Readers, if you don't get this, if you still think *Conviction* is fundamentally a legal drama about DNA evidence, motions and appeals, then I suggest you go back and see it again.

© Jan Lisa Huttner (11/2/10)—Special for WomenArts

The Devil Wears Prada
Directed by David Frankel
Screenplay by Aline Brosh McKenna
(based on a novel by Lauren Weisberger)

Principal Actors: Anne Hathaway
with Meryl Streep and Adrian Grenier

Beneath the glitter of the clothes and the jewels and all the perks of limoed life, The Devil Wears Prada *is, in fact, a highly realistic depiction of a female executive, probably the most realistic depiction ever filmed. Yes, Streep embodies Miranda to perfection, but primary credit here goes to director David Frankel and screenwriter Alice Brosh McKenna. They've made Prada so much fun to watch that many people don't even realize what they're really seeing.*

Penny's Points: ✳✳✳✳½

According to Karen Valby (writing about Meryl Streep on page 56 of the "Special Year-End Double Issue" of *Entertainment Weekly*), *The Devil Wears Prada* was last summer's "Cinderella story," (with world-wide box office grosses already over $300 million on a budget of $35M). But as the awards season heats up, all eyes remain on Streep, as if she's not just one of the greatest actors of her generation, but someone who also transcends her material – writing her own speeches, blocking her own scenes, and making everyone else on *Prada's* creative team simply superfluous.

This is, of course, ridiculous. Streep's brilliance (about which there is no question) didn't save *Prime, She-Devil,* or a great many other films in which she's starred, from critical and/or commercial oblivion. But ignoring *Prada's* creative team and focusing just on Streep's performance is nothing new; rather it's part of a well-documented pattern. Hilary Swank came out of nowhere to win the Best Actress Oscar for *Boys Don't Cry* in 1999, but when was the last time you heard any buzz about writer/director Kimberly Peirce? Charlize Theron received the Best Actress Oscar for *Monster* in 2003 after years of arm-candy roles, but when was the last time you heard any buzz about writer/director Patty Jenkins?

Rewarding the actress, as wonderful as she may be, typically goes hand-in-hand with trivializing the film in which she shines, especially when the film was written and/or directed by another woman. In 2003, *Frida* received six Oscar nominations (including one for Salma Hayek in the title role), but director Julie Taymor was slighted, even though Taymor was the first woman ever to win a Tony award for directing a Broadway musical *(The Lion King).* And this year Hollywood princess Sofia Coppola learned the lesson too: make a film that stars a man *(Lost in Translation)* and everyone applauds; make a film that stars a woman *(Marie Antoinette)* and you're yesterday's news. Like poor Rodney Dangerfield, films by women, especially when they're also films about women, just don't get no respect.

Does it take anything away from Streep if we sing her praises within the context of this film? Quite the contrary: as *Prada* makes clear to us, "Miranda Priestly" depends on her *Runway* magazine support staff every waking minute of every day. With *Prada* DVDs already on the shelf for all to see and the closing date for Academy Award nominations (1/13/07) imminent, there's just enough time for one more look before the envelopes are irrevocably sealed.

When *The Devil Wears Prada* arrived in bookstores in the spring of 2003, the cheeky little novel became an immediate chick-lit classic. Everyone in the biz knew that author Lauren Weisberger had once worked for Vogue editor Anna Wintour, so the book was read as a roman-a-clef, even though Weisberger herself was always careful to explain that "Miranda" had many different sources. The novel's protagonist is definitely "Andy Sachs" (a character loosely based on Weisberger although she's given herself a decidedly more upscale background).

Andy's life is filled with problems: she has problems with Jill (her sister), problems with Nate (her boyfriend), problems with Lily (her roommate/best friend), and oh yes, she also has problems with Miranda Priestly (her terrifying boss). Miranda takes Andy to Paris for Fashion Week only after Emily (Miranda's "first assistant") is ordered into bed by her physician, and Andy abandons Miranda in Paris because Lily's in the hospital. By novel's end, Andy is exploring her options as a freelance writer, selling-off her *Runway* magazine chum to consignment shops whenever she needs some extra pocket cash.

In the screen version of *Prada*, by contrast, Miranda Priestly is the sun in Andy's universe; Andy, Emily, Nigel (a composite of characters on the edges of the novel's action) and a Manhattan skyscraper filled with "clackers" (stringbeans in stiletto heels) orbit around Miranda and reflect her radiance. Keeping tight focus on the *Runway* world, the screenplay reduces Andy's family to one visit from Dad, turns Lily to a bit player, and houses Andy in a tiny tenement flat with Nate.

Prada the film then expands to explore the intricacies of Miranda's private life (details in which the novel's narrator has no interest). And here's the bottom line: Miranda Priestly is an ambitious working mother doing her best to raise twin daughters with an endless series of "father figures" who leave in a huff once they've been called "Mr. Priestly" one too many times in public. Barely adolescents, the daughters are already little witches, and Miranda, for all her worldly power, has absolutely none at home.

So beneath the glitter of the clothes and the jewels and all the perks of limoed life, *Prada* is, in fact, a highly realistic depiction of a female executive, probably the most realistic depiction ever filmed. Yes, Streep embodies Miranda to perfection, but primary credit here goes to director David Frankel and screenwriter Alice Brosh McKenna. They've made *Prada* so much fun to watch that many people don't even realize what they're really seeing. Frankel (the Emmy-winning son of Max Frankel, a former executive editor at the *New York Times*) and McKenna (who graduated magna cum lauda from Harvard) clearly know everything there is to know about East Coast Jewish workaholics, and it's that insider knowledge that enables them to pull the whole thing off with such elan.

Life at *Runway* magazine is like life in office towers all around the world, filled with competitive, aggressive young people from top schools who work horrendous hours under oppressive conditions, scratching and scheming to get ahead. Like Andy, most of these newbees will come to have second thoughts about the price of success, and very few of the people who will eventually inhabit corner offices will be women. Anyone who really wants to understand the world in which we live today would do well to take *Prada* very seriously. It addresses questions few of us have yet had the courage to ask.

© **Jan Lisa Huttner (12/31/06) —Special for Digital Filmmaker**

Divan
Documentary by Pearl Gluck

Key Participants: Pearl Gluck
with Pearl's Parents & Extended Family

Jewish intellectual from a Hasidic family creates a future for herself that honors her past even while acknowledging the pain & rage which result from being banished by traditionalists who reject her for her choices.

Penny's Points: ✳✳✳✳½

A film called *Divan* will be released on DVD this month after a successful run around the Jewish film festival circuit as well as some commercial bookings (including a week at Chicago's Landmark Century Theater). The narrator is Pearl Gluck, a Jewish-American woman on a quest of her own.

Pearl comes from a large Hasidic family based in the Borough Park neighborhood of Brooklyn. Unlike the more devout women in her family, however, Pearl finished college, began work on a doctorate in European Studies, and received a Fulbright Fellowship to collect the oral histories of Yiddish-speakers in Eastern Europe.

But her father thinks she's making all the wrong choices, so in an attempt to mollify him she makes a promise: while in Europe she will search for a precious heirloom, a divan that according to family legend served as the sleeping place for generations of prominent traveling rabbis.

Pearl's European adventures are straight-forward. She meets no doppelgangers, just aging relatives who never left Hungary, somehow managing to survive both Hitler and Stalin. She drives through the countryside with an elderly uncle, all the while discussing the difference between current borders and the borders of memory. (Same old story: This used to be Poland, but now it's Ukraine.)

Pearl finds the divan, but when she tries to bring it back to her father, relatives on distant continents make urgent phone calls to stop her. In the end, she finds a prize even more valuable than the one she went looking for, and she returns to Manhattan.

While this may sound heavy and serious, Pearl has a whimsical touch, and she counterpoints the travel scenes with the voices of Gen-Xers like herself who are also struggling to find a balance between the religious and the secular. Some of the friends Pearl interviews are noteworthy in their own right (like Basya Schechter of the band *Pharaoh's Daughter),* some less so. But all are articulate and engaging. The glue is provided by a fabulous soundtrack by prolific composer Frank London, best known for his work with the Klezmatics.

Pearl Gluck is a *zamler* (the Yiddish word for "collector") who understands that seemingly ordinary objects can sometimes embody the sacred.

© Jan Lisa Huttner (9/01/05)—Special for World Jewish Digest

Elegy
Directed by Isabel Coixet
Screenplay by Nicholas Meyer
(Based on Philip Roth's novel *The Dying Animal)*

Principal Actors: Sir Ben Kingsley
with Penelope Cruz & Dennis Hopper

New adaptation of Philip Roth's novel The Dying Animal *succeeds in capturing the author's humanity. Excellent cast is headlined by Ben Kinsley as*

"David Kepesh" (a serial seducer who becomes obsessed with a beautiful young woman), and Penelope Cruz as "Consuela" (someone longing for safe harbor after disappointments of her own). Dennis Hopper is cast against type as the buddy who seems to walk lightly around the edges of Kepesh's life, but is actually the one who helps keep him connected. Someday we'll all be gone, but new people will likely still be around to appreciate the works of art we've left behind.

Penny's Points: ✷✷✷✷½

Something wonderful has happened to Philip Roth's career in the past decade, and I don't just mean the fact that he's continuing to publish novels that are both critically acclaimed and financially successful well into his senior years. As a film critic (a film critic born and raised in the Weequahic section of Newark, NJ!), I'm delighted to report that he's finally found filmmakers looking for the humanity in his work and not just the misogyny.

When *The Human Stain* was released in 2003, it landed in the number two spot on my yearend "Ten Best" list, and I still think it's a terrific example of a film that's better than its source book. (For more on this, see comments below.) But good as *The Human Stain* is, I think *Elegy,* based on Roth's 2001 novel *The Dying Animal,* is even better. This time Lakeshore Entertainment, the producers of *The Human Stain*, have placed screenwriter Nicholas Meyer's latest adaptation in the hands of Spanish director Isabel Coixet, and her stitching is seamless.

Elegy is the story of Public Radio guru "David Kepesh" (Ben Kingsley), a man-about-town who still does some teaching and some writing, but no longer has any interest in serious scholarship. He's certainly Jewish, but his life has no visibly Jewish elements and his role as a public intellectual doesn't tilt him in any way towards overtly Jewish themes or topics.

As the film begins, Kepesh is living a sublimely unencumbered life: he owns a tastefully furnished home in Manhattan; he shares his bed with a beautiful but highly independent woman named "Carolyn" (Patricia Clarkson); and he keeps in shape by playing squash with his simpatico buddy "George" (Dennis Hopper). Years before, Kepesh fathered a son and then left him to be raised by an embittered ex-wife. Now the adult "Kenny" (Peter Sarsgaard) is filled with rage, so Kepesh is careful to maintain his emotional distance. The ugly stories Kenny heard from his mother are all true, so why deny them? Kepesh is a serial seducer, and his classrooms are the private feeding grounds of a shark on the hunt.

Then a new semester begins, in walks "Consuela" (Penelope Cruz), and all the air goes out of his inflated ego. Consuela is reserved and elegant, and as soon as Kepesh succeeds in making love to her, he's instantly obsessed by the thought that one day she will leave him.

This man, David Kepesh, I know this man very well. I've met his type many times, at many different points in my own life. As a feminist, I hate him, and as a Jewish feminist, I actively despise him… and yet… and yet… By the end of *Elegy,* I found myself crying real tears for this man, a man terrified by illness and death, a man so afraid of being alone that he runs from every offer of genuine intimacy.

Coixet and Meyer both see into the soul of this man with great clarity, and Kingsley portrays their vision of him perfectly. He captures every nuance, as the worm of self-doubt reveals itself beneath the erudite charm and the healthy, albeit aging, body. Cruz, so loud and blowsy in recent films like *Volver* and *Vicky Christina Barcelona,* is appropriately introverted and refined here, and she's just old enough to be the right onscreen age for this Kepesh. She has little lines around her eyes that prove she's no longer a girl, and prior love affairs now cast tiny shadows of melancholia across her otherwise luminous face.

Clarkson and Sarsgaard are both extremely good in their parts, but they always are, and this particular film doesn't force either of them into new emotional territory. Dennis Hopper, on the other hand, is cast against type, and Coixet turns him into a genuine mentsch. I've just scrolled through his enormous profile on the Internet Movie Database, and I can't think of another time Hopper has played a role as sweet-tempered and worldly-wise as this one. To round out George's character, Coixet and Meyer have also crafted a small part for *Blondie* singer Deborah Harry (as George's wife "Amy"), and brief as it is, her one scene with Kingsley creates an emotional launch pad for the film's final act.

The critic who saw this film left the screening room a better woman, someone with just a bit more compassion and insight, someone with more respect than ever for the artist who fights mano-a-mano with the grim reaper and wins.

SPOILER ALERT!!!
Please do NOT read until AFTER you have seen *Elegy*

Although I cover all Jewish culture topics in my monthly *JUF News* column "Tzivi's Spotlight," I think of myself primarily as a film critic. Therefore, when I know (or guess) that a filmmaker is interested in adapting a specific novel for the screen, I make a personal vow **NOT** to read the book until I've seen the film. The simple truth is that even an unsuccessful film typically has an audience that is larger – often by many magnitudes – than the readership of a best-selling book. So I want to judge the material as most of my own readers will: film first.

But after I've seen a film, I often read the source material, especially if I either love the film (recent examples include *Beaufort* and *The Namesake),* or I feel in my gut that the adaptation is a bad one (recent examples include *Atonement* and *There Will Be Blood).*

I definitely do **NOT** believe that the source book is **ALWAYS** better than the film. I can name several films which are actually better than their source books. Two of my favorite examples are *The Cider House Rules* and *Fugitive Pieces*. In other cases, the film and the source book run parallel, so that each one actually enhances the other. *Beaufort* and *The Namesake* are both good examples of this.

As I already said in my review (above), I think *The Human Stain* is a terrific example of a film that's better than its source book. When John Irving, adapting his own novel, eliminated the "Melony" character from his Oscar-winning screenplay for *The Cider House Rules,* it was a necessary cut, but I'm sure it was painful for him, and I know for a fact that many readers missed her. On the other hand, I think director Robert Benton was extremely wise to ignore all the venomous pages Roth devoted to his caricature of Coleman Silk's academic nemesis "Delphine Roux." The noxious Professor Roux has been respectably repackaged for the screen, and she appears defanged, embodied by classy-looking actress Mimi Kuzyk, in only one brief faculty meeting.

From the feminist perspective, *The Dying Animal* is blessedly short of misogynistic excess, and there was only one scene in the novel that made me sigh and put my book aside for a few minutes. Perhaps Coixet felt the same way, because there's no hint of this scene in the film…

The Dying Animal is the third of Philip Roth's three books about David Kepesh, but there's a big gap between this one and the first two *(The Breast* and *The Professor of Desire),* and Roth never invested Kepesh with the diachronic dimensionality he's lavished on his Newark-born alter ego "Nathan Zuckerman." (Note that Zuckerman is the narrator of the Coleman Silk story Roth tells in *The Human Stain.)*

The Dying Animal is a first-person narrative. Readers have no independent source of information about Carolyn, Consuela, George or Kenny; we only know what David Kepesh tells us, and everything he says about them inevitably comes from his own point-of-view. In *Elegy,* on the other hand, all these characters come to life.

- The dialogue in the Kepesh/George scenes is masterful, and I love the fraternal quality of their on screen relationship. (Roth devotees know that Kepesh was an only child from reading *The Professor of Desire,* so it feels right to make George a brother as much as a friend.)

- Kenny's not a physician in the novel, but giving him this role in the film helps in two ways: it gives Kepesh someone to go to for medical information when he learns about Consuela's illness; and it allows Kenny to finally grow-up and interact with his father as an adult.

- Finally, the novel's Consuela is considerably younger than her on screen persona, and this is a tremendous improvement. When Kepesh refuses to attend her graduation party, the implications for a Consuela in her early 20's are not the same as the implications for a Consuela in her late 20's or early 30's. (Cruz is actually 34, and she's earned her looks. In *Volver,* Almodóvar cast her as the mother of a teenager.)

By and large though, while they "speak for themselves" now, their essential character arcs all remain very close to the ones Roth originally created for each of them.

But there's one beautiful bit in the film that is not in the novel. Kepesh is doing a live radio interview with an art historian, and their conversation is a perfect encapsulation. It reminded me of the terrific line Meyer wrote for *The Human Stain,* when Anna Deavere Smith as young Coleman's mother says to him: "I never thought of you as Black or White; to me, you were always my Golden child." I'm willing to bet that, come what may this

November, Meyer's line will reappear one day in a Barack Obama biopic. Maybe Wentworth Miller (who played young Coleman) is already working on it!

© **Jan Lisa Huttner (8/21/08) —Special for WomenArts**

The Governess
Written & Directed by Sandra Goldbacher

Principal Actors: Minnie Driver
with Tom Wilkinson & Harriet Walter

This film takes Charlotte Bronte's classic Jane Eyre *and turns it inside-out and upside-down. When Rosina de Silva's father is murdered under mysterious circumstances, he leaves the family with debts no one anticipated. Rosina is secretly thrilled by the prospect of adventure, and using her fine-tuned theatrical imagination, she creates a new identity.*

Penny's Points: ✳✳✳✳½

The Internet Movie Database classifies *The Governess* as a "Romance," and most reviewers concur, caught up in the period dress of the Mary-Charles-Henry triangle. But "surface" is the very question addressed by this film rather than its answer. Right from the opening act, Director Goldbacher is announcing that things are never what they seem to be. Rosina's father has created a solid, respectable exterior, but Rosina crosses the threshold from child to woman at the moment she realizes she has no idea who her father really was.

Charles Cavendish's laboratory is strictly off-limits to everyone, but Rosina sneaks in anyway and is immediately fascinated by the potential of his photographic research. Charles thinks he's capturing reality, but Rosina knows otherwise. She intuitively understands that subjects can be posed and objects can be arranged. For Rosina, the science of photography is only a means to the goal of aesthetic expression.

The name Sandra Goldbacher was new to me the first time I saw this film. I only knew I was entranced by the sensuous cinematography and mesmerized by the hypnotic score. (Rosina's family is Sephardic, so her music is a world away from the Ashkenazy klezmer we typically think of as ethnic "Jewish music.") I knew I was watching an overtly feminist film, but I was held in thrall by the actors: Minnie Driver's beauty is ripe, and Tom Wilkinson (as Charles Cavendish) has never had a role this virile before.

Now I know that Sandra Goldbacher is an acclaimed director, well-known in Britain for her television commercials and BBC documentaries. *The Governess*, her first feature film, was nominated for numerous awards at multiple European film festivals, (The cinematographer, Ashley Rowe, won the Evening Standard British Film Award.) Only in America, it seems, was this film simply dismissed as a lady's gothic.

Some films demand multiple viewings, and this is certainly one of them. For a beautifully written, academically-oriented discussion of the groundbreaking significance of *The Governess* check out "Capturing the Shadows of Ghosts: Mixed Media and the Female Gaze" by Lynette Felber in the Summer 2001 issue of *Film Quarterly* (Volume 54, Number 4).

© **Jan Lisa Huttner (6/28/02)—Special for DVDWolf**

The Hurt Locker
Directed by Kathryn Bigelow
Screenplay by Marc Boal

Principal Actors: Jeremy Renner
with Brian Geraghty & Anthony Mackie

Date: Summer 2004. Place: Iraq. Army Specialist Owen Eldridge (Brian Geraghty), Staff Sergeant William James (Jeremy Renner), and Sergeant J.T. Sanborn (Anthony Mackie) are members of an American EOD squad ("Explosive Ordinance Disposal") crisscrossing the streets of Baghdad in their humvee. The Hurt Locker *brackets out politics. Director Kathryn Bigelow and her team are totally focused on putting us in the boots of an EOD squad and showing us the world through their eyes. She has done her job, now we must do ours.*

Penny's Points: ✳✳✳✳½

Heat! My two favorite Kathryn Bigelow films—*Point Break* and *The Weight of Water*—taught me new respect for the ocean: huge waves crashing against the northern edge of Australia; furious storms lashing the rocky islands off New Hampshire. In her new film, *The Hurt Locker,* the Iraqi heat feels so intense that I'm sweating. I'm sitting in the cool darkness of a Chicago screening room, but grit prickles my throat and my eyes ache from the sun's relentless glare.

The Hurt Locker brackets out politics. Perhaps Americans should never have sent soldiers to Iraq, but the fact is we did. Bigelow honors their service by placing us in their boots, giving us an opportunity to literally see the world through their eyes.

The three main characters in *The Hurt Locker* are members of an EOD squad ("Explosive Ordinance Disposal"). A routine patrol spots something "suspicious." Maybe a car is parked somewhere it shouldn't be, or a pile of rubbish has wires sticking out of it, or something just looks "wrong." Time stops. The soldiers call for an EOD squad, establish a perimeter, evacuate civilians, and wait.

Army Specialist Owen Eldridge, Staff Sergeant William James, and Sergeant J.T. Sanborn crisscross the streets of Baghdad in their humvee ("High Mobility Multipurpose Wheeled Vehicle"), responding to calls. Day after day after day, they, and only they, cross the perimeter. Their job is to make things right… or die trying.

EOD squads are elite units, so Eldridge, James, and Sanborn have volunteered for hazardous duty twice, first by joining the Army and then by requesting EOD training. They have each traveled a different path to reach their first moment of shared crisis, but there are no flashbacks to fill in past lives. Everything is in the moment, and as bomb after bomb is defused, we learn intimate secrets about camaraderie, courage, and honor.

Sergeant J.T. Sanborn (Anthony Mackie) spent seven years in Intelligence before moving to the EOD squad. He has a mature personality anchored by considerable military experience. When they reach a new site, Sanborn is the man who stays closest to the humvee, steering his team members while also communicating with the other soldiers on the scene.

Army Specialist Owen Eldridge (Brian Geraghty) is the rookie. His job is to eliminate potential trouble coming from outside the perimeter. Sanborn, look to the right! Someone on the balcony has a cell phone! Sanborn, look to the left! Someone on the roof has a camera! Is one of these (or both) a triggering device!?!

Staff Sergeant William James (Jeremy Renner) is the man actually responsible for defusing bombs. Every situation starts the same way. The humvee arrives at the perimeter and Sanborn helps James suit up. Like an astronaut or a deep sea diver or a knight in shining armor, James must be completely encased in protective gear before he can begin to do his job. Hot! So hot! Suiting up in the heat of day is James' first act of courage, even before he begins his perilous walk towards the IED ("Improvised Explosive Device").

Whatever life trajectory brought each man to this specific point in time, Eldridge, James, and Sanborn all respond to the moment with a unique combination of training and temperament. And with each incident, Bigelow pushes us ever deeper into the emotional complexity of 21st Century war. Pundits and historians can debate causes and consequences, but for filmmaker Kathryn Bigelow there's only one side—side-by-side with the soldiers.

Brian Geraghty ("Eldridge"), Anthony Mackie ("Sanborn"), and Jeremy Renner ("James") are not well-known actors, but I've seen them all in numerous prior films, and all three of them go way beyond their previous personal bests here, creating indelible characters with superlative chemistry. In every scene, they each dig deep, revealing subtle backstory and increasing complexity as individuals as well as team members. Every line reading, gesture, and grimace works. No false moments. No wrong steps.

That said, the real star of *The Hurt Locker* is English cinematographer Barry Ackroyd, who uses his significant documentary experience to ground the action, capturing multiple points-of-view by simultaneously filming from various angles with numerous hand-held cameras. Somehow editors Bob Murawski and Chris Innis meticulously stitched all this footage together, expertly locating us within the physical danger and emotional turmoil of each scene. Triangulation at every moment is critical: where is the character, where is the IED; where is the perimeter. I suspect this was Bigelow's most important directive to every member of her team.

Close to perfect, *The Hurt Locker* does have one major flaw. Specifically, almost all of the action is set in the city of Baghdad, but suddenly, in one scene, Eldridge, James, and Sanborn are in the desert. The psychodynamic and technical components of this scene are just as well-crafted as the rest of the film, but with no explanation of how they got there, it just doesn't fit. Even so, *The Hurt Locker* is by far the best film to date about the Iraq War, and it takes its place with *Beaufort, Das Boot, Full Metal Jacket, Lawrence of Arabia, Patton,* and *Twelve O'Clock High* as one of the best combat films ever made.

****

Can We Talk?
Three Reasons Why YOU Should See *The Hurt Locker*

The Hurt Locker has received incredibly positive reviews from a great many critics (including women as well as men). As of today (7/7/09), *The Hurt Locker's Rotten Tomato* score is 95% "Fresh" (http://www.rottentomatoes.com/m/hurt_locker). But since I'm writing this review for a website targeted to women, I'd like to use this opportunity to tell women everywhere why WE (each and every one of us) should see this film.

1.) I can already hear some of you saying you don't like violence and you consciously avoid films that you know will be violent. Believe me, I understand! I also abhor gratuitous violence! *The Hurt Locker* is about bomb disposal, so no question about it, *The Hurt Locker* is a violent film that contains several massive explosions as critical plot elements. So why am I emphatically telling you to please go anyway?

The simple fact is that violence is a part of life and although I abhor gratuitous violence, I also applaud filmmakers who take violence on as a serious narrative subject. *The Hurt Locker* is about the war in Iraq, and one of the distinguishing features of this specific conflict is insurgent use of IEDs. Even today, IEDs kill massive numbers of Iraqi men, women, and children, so every time EOD squad members destroy an IED, they help save the lives of countless Americans and Iraqis. In the moral equation of the Iraq War, EOD squad members are definitely good guys, and we should honor their service on our behalf accordingly.

2.) Relatively few women have direct military experience, but many of us vote for politicians who make decisions with military consequences, therefore I believe it is extremely important for women to seek experiential understanding of military realities. A film like *The Hurt Locker* offers us a chance to walk a mile in military boots with total personal safety. It may be the only chance many of us get. As wives, mothers, and friends, we owe it to the men in our lives; as voters, we owe it to ourselves.

While I'm on this subject, I should mention that another distinguishing feature of the War in Iraq is the relatively large presence of women in combat and support roles (including the appearance of women's names and photos in stateside death lists). Therefore, I am a bit surprised that Kathryn Bigelow didn't show any female combatants in *The Hurt Locker,* even though she has created powerful women characters in almost all of her prior films. There are no female characters in *Lawrence of Arabia* and it's still my all-time favorite film, so this is not a criticism of *The Hurt Locker,* just an observation.

3.) In 81 years of Oscar history, only three women have ever been nominated for a Best Director Oscar (Lena Wertmuller, Jane Campion, and Sofia Coppola) and no woman has ever received a Best Director Oscar. Now that Barack Obama is President and the Iraq War appears to be winding down, I believe Americans are ready for a strong film about Iraq. So far, the narrative films made about the Iraq War have been well-intentioned but fairly weak (e.g., *In the Valley of Elah, Stop Loss,* etc.), but *The Hurt Locker* is a very powerful film.

I sincerely believe that only one thing stands between Kathryn Bigelow and a Best Director nomination: box office. Critical buzz is already very strong, so if *The Hurt Locker* generates respectable box office returns, then Kathryn Bigelow will receive an Oscar nomination. So, women: we hold this in our hands. If we turn out for *The Hurt Locker,* (if we use our "power of the purse"), we can help Kathryn Bigelow become the 4th woman in history nominated for a Best Director Oscar. And if this happens, if Kathryn Bigelow receives a nomination, I also believe there's a good chance she will then become the first woman in history to actually receive a Best Director Oscar.

Now, I suspect Kathryn Bigelow would find this addendum very annoying. She doesn't want to be known as "a woman filmmaker," she doesn't want to answer questions about how her gender affects her POV, and she wants people to see her film on its own merits (that is, she would NOT want you to see *The Hurt Locker* just because it's directed by a woman). But I'm putting myself on record anyway, because I sincerely believe there is more at stake here than the cost of a movie ticket, distress at on-screen violence, or any other reason you might have for NOT going. Kathryn Bigelow has put *The Hurt Locker* out there for all to see, and I urge each and every one of YOU to see it in a movie theatre as soon as you can!

Kathryn Bigelow has done her job, now we must do ours.

© **Jan Lisa Huttner (7/7/09)—Special for WomenArts**

In a Better World
Directed by Susanne Bier
Screenplay by Anders Thomas Jensen

Principal Actors: Mikael Persbrandt
with William Jøhnk Nielsen & Markus Rygaardy

"Anton," the central character in Susanne Bier's Oscar-winning film In a Better World, *is a physician who divides his time between the comforts of Denmark and the rigors of an African refugee camp. Although surrounded by poverty and hardship, Anton knows who he is in Africa. He does his job and most days he wins: the sick are healed; the weak are restored. But as soon as Anton returns home, the skies above him turn dark and cloudy, and daily life is suddenly much more complicated.*

How does a good man, a modern man, a 21st Century "First World" man with all of his privileges teach his son to walk the line between mensch and wimp? This is the moral dilemma posed by In a Better World. *Anton takes his responsibilities as a role model seriously, but his son "Elias" is already old enough to see the harsh realities of life for himself, and the story has a spiral structure that forces its parallel characters towards an ever narrowing set of options. As a feminist, I don't often feel that women have an easier time in the world, but I definitely had a new appreciation of the complexities of masculinity after watching* In a Better World.

Penny's Points: ✳✳✳✳½

Two schoolboys meet in a seemingly idyllic Danish classroom. The new kid is "Christian" (William Jøhnk Nielsen); his seatmate is "Elias" (Markus Rygaard).

Christian has been living in London where his father "Claus" (Ulrich Thomsen) works. His mother has recently died of cancer, and father and son have returned home, at least temporarily, to live with Claus' mother "Signe" (Elsebeth Steentoft).

Elias lives with his mother "Marianne" (Trine Dyrholm) and his younger brother "Morten" (Toke Lars Bjarke). Elias' father

"Anton" (Mikael Persbrandt) is a physician who also works abroad, dividing his time between the comforts of Denmark and the rigors of an African refugee camp.

We all want to believe in utopia; we all want to think that with enough time, effort, education, patience, whatever, we can make the world a perfect place, but, alas, it's not so simple. Young as they are, Christian and Elias already know the world is full of bullies, especially that ultimate bully Death—the Grim Reaper. (Since this is a Scandinavian film, the image of "Antonius Block," the chess-playing knight in Ingmar Bergman's masterpiece *The Seventh Seal,* seems to haunt the edge of the frame.)

So what is the good man, the modern man, the 21st Century "First World" man with all of his privileges to do? In the face of these realities, how will he teach his son to walk the line between mensch and wimp? This is the moral dilemma posed by director Susanne Bier and screenwriter Anders Thomas Jensen in their latest collaboration *In a Better World.*

The central character in *In a Better World* is Anton, initially presented to us as an archetypal hero: a white European male calmly performing emergency surgeries and dispensing medicines in a field hospital. "How are you? How are you?" cry an adoring throng of Black youngsters every time his jeep arrives from the base camp. Tired as he is, Anton's face shines with self-satisfaction. He knows who he is in Africa. He does his job and most days he wins: the sick are healed; the weak are restored.

When Anton returns home, however, the sky above him immediately turns dark and cloudy. The same wind that blows aimlessly over the parched earth of Africa has been harnessed in Denmark; huge blades capture it and use it to maintain the landscape's luxurious green carpet. But his wife Marianne greets him coldly. She thought they had a perfect marriage; she was wrong. Anton has been cheating on her, and now she cannot forgive him for her own self-deception.

Despite her ambivalence, however, Marianne still wants her sons to love their father. Furthermore, Elias has been having problems in school, and Marianne thinks Anton's presence will make things better. Once again, Marianne is naïve.

Long after he knew the facts, Claus kept telling Christian that his mother could beat her cancer. And so Christian, already alert to adult lies, sees through Anton's facade after an altercation with a local bully named "Lars" (Kim Bodnia). Anton wants the boys to dismiss Lars as a mere nuisance rather than a threat, but Christian convinces Elias that they must redeem Anton's lost honor, and so they hunt Lars down and plot their revenge.

The story has a spiral structure that forces its parallel characters towards an ever narrowing set of options. Two fathers strive to be good role models, "civilized" men coping as best they can with the vagaries of modern life, but two boys see the harsh realities that lie beneath these empty reassurances. There are bullies everywhere who will not contain their behavior; bullies who test themselves against the rules just to see if they're strong enough to break them. That this film ends more or less happily, after so much dread, is part of the illusion: when all is said and done, our only option is to keep trying. There is no other choice.

Even though *In a Better World* was directed by a woman, the world that director Susanne Bier depicts on screen is definitely a man's world. Christian has idealized his mother, but in his heart he knows she was no saint, and his grandmother Signe is unable to comfort him. Marianne is closer to her boys, but also completely ineffectual when Elias needs her the most.

As a feminist, I don't often feel that women have an easier time in the world, but I definitely felt that way watching this film.

Men are more hierarchical than women (seemingly always forced to measure themselves on some new "alpha dog" scale), so most women don't have the same relation to evil that men have. Furthermore there's truth to the adage that "men act out whereas women act in," therefore disputes between women rarely become as deadly and literally life-threatening as disputes between men. "Honor" means more to men than to women, and there are codes of masculinity in all cultures that acknowledge this.

In 2009, Mikael Persbrandt was named Best Actor by the Swedish Film Institute, rewarded with a Guldbagge Award for playing "Siggy Larsson" in Jan Troell's film *Everlasting Moments.* Ironically the Siggy of *Everlasting Moments* is exactly the kind of abusive bully that Anton must confront in *In a Better World,* but he is so transformed as Anton that I had no sense of ever having seen him onscreen before. Bier uses Persbrandt's robust physique to her advantage, and Persbrandt's performance is heart-rending precisely because he must always struggle to contain his obvious strength and power. If only being a man was simply a matter of muscle.

Beyond the excellent cast, I was particularly moved by Morten Søborg's elegant cinematography which captures the heat of Africa in counterpoint to the cool of Denmark. Tracking dust devils (mini-tornadoes made of sand) at the edges of the camp, Anton shades his eyes from the glare. Back home he's surrounded by water, sometimes diving in head first to cool his roiling emotions. I also loved Johan Söderqvist's subtle soundtrack which augments the action and never overpowers it.

In a Better World received the 2011 Oscar in the Best Foreign Language Film category as well as the Golden Globe. At this point I've seen three of the other candidates on each list (including Alejandro González Iñárritu's film *Biutiful* which also appears on both lists), so I haven't seen them all yet, but I'm still very happy with this choice.

After I saw *In a Better World* the first time, I left the screening room and called my husband, thanking him for always trying as hard as he does to be a mensch in all circumstances regardless of provocation (sometimes even from me). I said this sincerely, with new appreciation. The second time I saw *In a Better World*, I saw it with him, and I'm proud to say he likes it too.

© **Jan Lisa Huttner (4/15/11)—Special for WomenArts**

Jane Eyre
Directed by Cary Fukunaga
Screenplay by Moira Buffini
(Based on a novel by Charlotte Brontë)

Principal Actors: Mia Wasikowska
with Jamie Bell & Michael Fassbender

A heroine created in the Victorian Era has indelibly imprinted herself on our cultural imagination. Director Cary Fukunaga has deliberately created his Jane Eyre *for the art house crowd, with a visual design completely committed to austere authenticity. Standing at a crossroads, all four directions equally bleak, Our Jane, in her simple dress, has hair wrapped tight around her head, and there's no trace of make-up on her pale, thin face. If you're looking for "realism," here it is.*

Penny's Points: ✳✳✳✳½

Director Cary Fukunaga has deliberately created his *Jane Eyre* for the art house crowd. Our Jane, wearing the same simple dresses day after day, has hair wrapped tight around her head, and there's no trace of make-up on her pale, thin face. But the cinematography is exquisite, beautifully used to establish mood as well as location. If you're looking for "realism," here it is.

When we first meet her, Jane is in flight, running from unnamed sorrows. A tiny figure set against the vast rugged moors of Northern England, she stands alone at a crossroads, and all four directions look equally bleak. The skies above her are filled with huge clouds which block the sun and eventually bring forth torrential rains. What has brought her to this desolate state and how can she ever survive it?

Flashbacks take us to dark and gloomy interiors; shadows engulf large rooms lit by tiny candles, and even when it's summer outside, a persistent chill mocks all the logs we see burning in fireplaces. Even if you haven't read Brontë's novel, or seen any of the numerous film and television adaptations, you can guess most of the backstory. Jane is an orphan cast off by rich relatives and sent to a boarding school one small step above a Dickensian workhouse. Fukunaga doesn't spend much time on any of this because he knows he doesn't need to; a few quick childhood scenes and Jane is already an adult eager to make her own choices.

Her first choice is to seek employment, and that leads her to Thornfield Hall, a large estate owned by one Edward Rochester and run by his distant relative Mrs. Fairfax. It's probably not that far, as the crow flies, from Lowood School to Thornfield Hall, but Jane has lead a sheltered life; she knows nothing at all about these people and precious little about their way of life. Mrs. Fairfax drops ominous hints about Mr. Rochester's past, but the only thing in evidence is a small girl named Adele. Mrs. Fairfax has hired Jane to be Adele's governess.

One day Mrs. Fairfax finds Jane on the balcony gazing across the parapet. She's bored by her surroundings and frustrated by her circumstances. Then Mr. Rochester arrives, bringing echoes of the outside world into Thornfield with him. He has little interest in the old woman and even less in the child, so he condescends to talk to the governess, ordering her (as an employer) to entertain him, and daring her (as a man) to amuse him.

Jane's pulse begins to quicken, but soon something else in the house demands Mr. Rochester's attention. Finding herself wrapped ever tighter in a spider's web of lies, Jane finally flees, and now we're all caught up and ready to begin Act Three.

Unlike most other film directors who've told this tale, Fukunaga is genuinely interested in what happens to Jane once she's gone over the wall. Standing perplexed at the crossroads, she finally picks a direction and sticks to it, slogging on in a cruel and dangerous world, until she finally finds both a new job and a new home.

Then problems come to the boil again when a seemingly suitable young man wants to marry her. She has not chosen St. John Rivers, but he has chosen her. She is tired. Her courageous heart falters. Maybe it's best to lean on St. John and let him make the big decisions about her future?

Jane's problem is a problem every young person must face: whom can she trust? In the end, Jane learns to trust her instincts, stay faithful to those who truly care for her, and keep her distance from those who would use her for their own purposes. Can any girl do more?

Mia Wasikowska (pronounced "Vash-i-kov-ska") anchors the film as "Jane", her first genuine leading role after superlative supporting performances in *Defiance* (2008), *That Evening Sun* (2009), and *The Kids Are All Right* (2010). True, she also played "Alice" in Tim Burton's *Alice in Wonderland* (2010), but that was a special effects extravaganza with no real commitment to character development. Wasikowska is a beautiful young woman who makes herself outwardly plain, so that all of Jane's curiosity, natural intelligence, and banked passion can come pouring through her eyes.

Jane's two suitors are both played by very accomplished actors. Jamie Bell (as "St. John Rivers") literally leapt to stardom in

2000, winning a BAFTA in his very first screen role as teenage dancer *"Billy Elliott."* He's been a fine Indie lead since, most notably in *The Chumscrubber* (2005) and *Mister Foe* (2007), and he's also been a strong supporting player in multiplex films like *King Kong* (2006), *Flags of our Fathers* (2007), and *The Eagle* (2010). In 2008, Bell played "Asael," the younger brother of Tuvia and Zus Bielski (Daniel Craig and Liev Schreiber) in Edward Zwick's *Defiance* (a relatively large role), whereas Wasikowska played Bell's wife "Chaya" (a small but memorable role).

By contrast, Michael Fassbender (who is a full decade older than Bell), has worked primarily on television. In 2008, however, he played IRA activist "Bobby Sands" in *Hunger* (a film I called "labored and abstract"), and in 2009, he played the seductive rake "Connor" in *Fish Tank* (a film I absolutely love). He also had a supporting role in *Inglorious Basterds* (2009), but I can barely remember it. "Edward Rochester" may be Fassbender's breakthrough role for mainstream audiences, but I'm frankly not convinced yet that he has the chops to play a romantic lead.

There are very few scenes in *Jane Eyre* not dominated by one of these three actors, but Judi Dench adds gravitas to "Mrs. Fairfax" (someone who suspects things she is unable to verbalize in part because of her role as Mr. Rochester's employee and in part because of her own limited knowledge of the world outside Thornhill), and Sally Hawkins is chilling as "Mrs. Reed" (the aunt who sends Jane off to Lowood).

In one of *Jane Eyre*'s best scenes, Mrs. Reed summons Jane to her deathbed, but why? Jane craves a tender moment and maybe some kind of apology; she even offers to forgive her aunt, but Mrs. Reed wants none of it. Hawkins regards Wasikowska with the cold eye of a shark: Jane has cursed the Reed family, and now Mrs. Reed demands that Jane own the results.

Bottom line: I enjoyed this look back at Victorian times very much. I found most of the acting and all of the cinematography both aesthetically and emotionally satisfying, and once again I marveled at how, by articulating the constraints faced by the women of her own era, Charlotte Brontë had paved the way for mine.

SPOILER ALERT!!!
Please do NOT read until AFTER you have seen *Jane Eyre*

Jane Eyre is a long novel well over 300 pages long, therefore many plot elements must be removed to craft a coherent screenplay.

Two points about this adaptation of *Jane Eyre*:

Screenwriter Moira Buffini made a brilliant call when she decided to open the film with Jane in full flight, minimizing the chapters about Jane's childhood and restoring St. John Rivers to a major player in the narrative—which he emphatically is not in most other versions. (Note that I'm only comparing feature length films here; made-for- television miniseries with multiple episodes have totally different structural requirements.)

The early image of Jane at the crossroads is definitive, making it clear that in this version of *Jane Eyre*, our heroine is a person who insists on making her own life choices regardless of the consequences. Charlotte Brontë surely knew she was writing at a time when few women thought they had such rights, and this alone makes Jane a radically new creature in English literature.

What Buffini jettisons is Brontë's attack on the clergy. I don't miss scenes of Mr. Brocklehurst's insidious behavior at Lowood (starving young girls in God's name and hacking off their curls with huge, monstrous scissors), but without this background, it's hard to understand why Jane is always so guarded around St. John Rivers. When St. John asks Jane to marry him and travel with him to India, the news of his intention to become a missionary comes totally out of the blue, whereas in the novel, St. John has been studying "Hindoostanee" with Jane's assistance for months, testing her thoroughly before proposing.

I appreciate that Jane returns to Mr. Rochester because she loves him. I applaud the fact that she has a choice of husbands and she exercises that choice freely at the end. I understand that love is ultimately a mystery and no one can predict who will set one's heart aflutter. But for all that, what I actually felt was that Wasikowska had more chemistry with Bell than with Fassbender, therefore this Jane only returned to this Rochester because this screenplay demanded it.

© **Jan Lisa Huttner (3/18/11)—Special for WomenArts**

Julie & Julia
Written & Directed By Nora Ephron
(Based on Julie Powell's book *Julie and Julia: My Year of Cooking Dangerously)*

Principal Actors: Amy Adams & Meryl Streep with Chris Messina & Stanley Tucci

Blogger Julie Powell works in a cubicle in an office overlooking Ground Zero, and the 9/11 tragedy is an omnipresent fact of her life. But instead of wallowing, she decides to sit herself down at the feet of a master and study her way up from horror to happiness. Ephron has created a loving tribute to teachers (and students) everywhere.

Penny's Points: ✳✳✳✳½

Cooking can be very comforting, especially at the end of a hard day (or a long week of them). Chopping, stirring, mashing— these can all be surprisingly relaxing activities, especially when the air fills with rich smells and you know your goal is to nurture those you love. Best yet, once you're done, you're done. Whatever tasted good, tasted good, and whatever didn't, well, that's life.

Julie Powell had a lot of hard days and long weeks in 2001. After the Twin Towers collapsed on 9/11, most of us went about our business, trauma fading into memory. But Julie Powell's job was to provide support for the families of 9/11 victims, and her office, looking out over Ground Zero, made tragedy an omnipresent fact of life. So instead of wallowing, this self-described "good student" did the obvious thing: she sat herself down at the feet of a master and literally studied her way up from horror to happiness.

The teacher: Julia Child.
The text: *Mastering the Art of French Cooking*.
The assignment: Make all 524 recipes in 365 days.

The first time I encountered Immanuel Kant's *Critique of Pure Reason* as a college Junior, I couldn't make any sense of it. Sighing deeply, my professor said: "Don't worry yourself so much, Miss Huttner. Many people have lived very happy lives without ever reading Kant." But to quote Mama Rose: "Some people ain't me!" I obsessed about Kant in graduate school, and ended up teaching a course on Kant's *Critique of Pure Reason* for the University of Chicago's Center on Continuing Education. So let's just say Nora Ephron's adaptation of Julie Powell's book *Julie & Julia: My Year of Cooking Dangerously* had me at hello.

Ephron starts her cinematic stew by blanching her leading lady before turning up the flame. She peels off Amy Adams' usual perky blonde cheerleader look, dressing her in ordinary, slightly ill-fitting clothes capped by a short, brownish, and very functional hair-do. The result is that Adams' eyes come to dominate her entire face, communicating enormous intelligence, as well as confusion, determination, elation, frustration, and the whole alphabet of emotions appropriate to events that unfold from the first day to the last day of "The Julie/Julia Project."

In 2005, Adams played "Ashley Johnsten" in the Indie drama *Junebug*. She won film festival awards (including a Special Jury Prize at Sundance) and she was nominated for an Oscar in the Best Supporting Actress category, but none of this hoopla resonated for me. However, her breakthrough role in *Junebug* lead to new opportunities, and I've been thoroughly charmed by Adams ever since. She's held the center with conviction in lead roles (e.g., *Enchanted* and *Sunshine Cleaning*), and she's also made delightful contributions in supporting roles (e.g., *Miss Pettigrew Lives for a Day* and *Night at the Museum: Battle of the Smithsonian*), all in parts that relied heavily on her looks. Even playing Sister James, the tormented nun in *Doubt* last year, Adams was luminous. Well, why not? She's beautiful and young! But playing Julie Powell transforms Adams from "starlet" to "pro." Now I can really see her developing into a great actress, carrying mature character roles in the recent tradition of Jessica Lange, Julianne Moore, Meryl Streep...

Wait! Did I just say Meryl Streep?!? Mountains of reviews have appeared since *Julie & Julia*'s nationwide release on August 7, most claiming two things: the star of *Julie & Julia* is Meryl Streep, and Meryl Streep plays Julia Child. Both of these assertions are false. *Julie & Julia* is not a biopic about "the real" Julia Child, and Meryl Streep isn't trying to embody "the real" Julia Child. The character Meryl Streep plays in *Julie & Julia* (as written and directed by Nora Ephron) is the personification of a great teacher: brilliant, enormously inspiring, and fully present in her work. Streep's role, in other words, is to be the Julia Child who lives in Julie Powell's head.

Of course Julie Powell's onscreen story seems drab and trivial compared to Julia Child's. That's not because Julia Child wrote one of the most influential cookbooks in American history, or because Julia Child was a television pioneer who helped bring PBS into the mainstream. It's not even because Julia Child is now a cultural icon whose Boston kitchen is preserved for posterity at the Smithsonian. In fact, these are the very reasons Julie Powell chose Julia Child as her personal life-preserver in the first place.

Perfectly capturing the underlying emotions in Powell's sourcebook, Ephron shows us the Julie who is constantly measuring herself against an idealized Julia. Julie can never measure up; she will always find herself wanting. But here's the thing: great teachers need great students, and just as Plato dedicated himself to Socrates, so Julie Powell dedicated herself to Julia Child. And bit by bit, under Julia Child's tutelage, Julie Powell became a better person—not just a better cook, but a more self-aware, self-confident person.

Adapting Powell's book for the big screen, Ephron has the tools at hand to turn Julie's dilemma into a wonderfully cinematic joke. Julia Child was famously tall (literally towering over everyone else in her life), but Meryl Streep isn't, so how did Ephron achieve this effect? Did her casting director roam around France looking for Munchkins? Who cares? It works—both visually and metaphorically. Under Ephron's direction, Streep rises before our eyes like a delicious soufflé.

And, oh yes: the real Julie Powell landed a book contract, and a movie deal, and can now see herself played onscreen by Amy Adams. The real Julia Child died too soon to see any of this happen, but I am absolutely certain that if Julia Child were standing with Julie Powell on the Red Carpet today, she would be very proud indeed.

Brava, Nora Ephron! With two great actresses and a superlative team, you've made a terrific film that's a tribute to teachers (and students) everywhere!

SPOILER ALERT: From Page to Screen
(Please do NOT read until after you have seen *Julie & Julia*)

As is my habit, I saw *Julie & Julia,* then I read Julie Powell's book, and then I saw *Julie & Julia* again before starting this review. So I knew nothing about Julie Powell, and almost nothing about Julia Child, when I formed my first impressions of Nora Ephron's film. Furthermore, I'm not a foodie; when I cook, I rely totally on gut instinct, keep things simple, and almost never consult recipes. I've never watched a cooking show, and any mental image I might have had of Julia Child before seeing *Julie & Julia* was heavily influenced by Dan Ackroyd's parody on *Saturday Night Live.*

Intentionally or not, Julie Powell keeps most of *Julie & Julia: My Year of Cooking Dangerously* in the present tense, and she tells us very little about her background. So I have no idea what brought "the real" Julie Powell and her husband Eric from Austin (where they were both raised) to Brooklyn (where they are living when the story begins). She talks a bit about theatre, but not too much.

The Julie character created by Nora Ephron, on the other hand, is a much more ambitious lady—someone who went to a first-class college and tried to write serious fiction before succumbing to financial imperatives. Ephron also gives her more accomplished friends, and more hands-on responsibility for solving the problems of 9/11 families. It is Ephron's Julie, not Powell's Julie, who tells husband Eric that she has always defined herself as a good student.

Julie Powell may not know this yet (after all, she's still very young), but Nora Ephron surely knows that the art of teaching, like all arts, is a dyadic activity; great teachers cannot reach their own potential without great students. So the character in her film is definitely a stronger, tougher, more competitive person than the character in Powell's book.

But the idealization of Julia Child—incomparable cook, perfect hostess, beloved wife—part Eiffel Tower and part Statue of Liberty—this character comes straight from Julie Powell, and she has earned the last words on the subject:

"I'd made eight French tarts, any one of which would have done me in a year ago. I'd had a dozen people over to my apartment, where a year ago I'd have been lucky to tempt two. Julia would be proud of me, if she knew, Hell, she *was* proud of me. I knew this because for nearly eleven months Julia had resided in my brain... She'd ensconced herself in there, so that now, though I couldn't look at her straight on without her melting away, I believed that she was with me more than I believed that she wasn't."

(Day 365; Recipe 524; Little, Brown and Company paperback page 313)

ONE FINAL POINT...

Something very weird is happening to Meryl Streep's career in mid-life, and it leaves a bitter aftertaste. Year after year, she draws us into her web with yet another superlative performance, at which point the critics rave, and then she's nominated for an Oscar. But the result is always the same. Critics use her brilliance to damn her collaborators (especially if they're female), and then, during awards season, she's invariably passed over.

Meryl Streep is quite simply the finest actress in screen history. There is no one (male or female) who can match her in the quality, quantity, depth, and range of her cinematic contributions. If I ruled the world, she would have received Best Actress Oscars for *Silkwood* (1983), *Out of Africa* (1986), *The Bridges of Madison County* (1995), *The Devil Wears Prada* (2006), and *Doubt* (2008). Last year's combination of *Doubt* and *Mama Mia* should have been more than sufficient, but in fact, Meryl Streep hasn't won an Oscar for twenty-six years! She received a Best Actress Oscar in 1983 for *Sophie's Choice,* and she also received a Best Supporting Actress Oscar in 1980 for *Kramer vs. Kramer.* That's it! Shameful!

So let's all agree that Meryl Streep is a great actress and let's reward her accordingly—but let's be clear here: Meryl Streep does not create her own characters; she does not write her own lines; she does not costume, light, or edit herself; and she's certainly not her own director. I shouldn't have to say this, but it seems, yet again, that I do.

© **Jan Lisa Huttner (8/11/09)—Special for WomenArts**

Lemon Tree (Etz Limon)
Directed by Eran Riklis
Screenplay by Riklis & Suha Arraf

Principal Actors: Hiam Abbass & Rona Lipaz-Michael

Salma Zidane is a Palestinian widow living in a small house on the eastern edge of the Green Line. Her life is immediately impacted when an Israeli woman named Mira Navon becomes her new neighbor. As they watch each other, day after day, from windows on opposite sides of the fence running through Salma's lemon grove, these two women become allies if never quite friends. Delicate and understated film has profound sympathy for female characters constrained by male conflicts.

Penny's Points: ✱✱✱✱½

"Salma Zidane," the main character in Eran Riklis's beautiful new film *Lemon Tree,* is a Palestinian widow who has lived in a small house on the eastern edge of the Green Line for most of her life. But Salma's quiet habits and lonely routines are immediately impacted when "Mira Navon" becomes her new neighbor. Mira and her husband are Israelis, and Mira's husband is Israel's minister of defense.

The trees that provide Salma with an income also provide cover for terrorists, so Navon's military minders decide to level the land on both sides of the fence separating their two homes. Salma receives a letter (in Hebrew) informing her she will be compensated, but when she asks her village elder to read it to her, he tells her she's not allowed to accept money from the Israeli government even when offered. With nothing to lose, Salma decides to fight back. She sells all her valuables and hires an attorney named "Ziad Daud."

Ziad has recently relocated to Ramallah, leaving an ex-wife and young daughter behind in Russia. He's ambitious and media-savvy, and he knows that representing Salma will enhance his reputation, both locally and internationally, even though he will almost certainly lose her case in court. Minister Navon, "Israel," is enraged; Ziad gets under his skin and the effort to appear reasonable on television makes him even more of a bully at home.

Salma and Mira are both empty-nesters with children in America, and as the film progresses, this becomes a source of mutual empathy. Watching from windows on different sides of Salma's lemon grove, they become allies if never quite friends. Mira doesn't consciously set out to betray Israel, but seeing how Salma responds under pressure makes Mira look inside herself for the first time in years. If Salma can resist, constrained as she is by expectations that are not in her own best interest, Mira realizes she can too.

Some people will come out of *Lemon Tree* thinking it's either pro-Palestinian and/or anti-Israeli but I disagree: director Eran Riklis doesn't provide any easy or polemical answers here. Riklis and screenwriter Suha Arraf (who also wrote *The Syrian Bride* screenplay with him) have developed a unique collaboration; their films are delicate and understated, with profound sympathy for female characters trapped at the edges of male conflict. When soldiers arrive to cut down Salma's trees, it's not just a power play. Terrorists are, in fact, hiding weapons in her lemon grove, and they have no more sympathy for Salma's predicament than her village elder does. She neither expects anything from them nor tries to defend them, and she knows from the start that even Ziad will ultimately betray her. By insisting on her day in court, Salma's not just protesting against Israeli occupation, she's also refusing to play by the rules of Palestinian society (seen here as always looking backwards and refusing to compromise).

Hiam Abbass plays Salma with enormous passion and dignity. I first became aware of Abbass when I saw her in *Satin Rouge* (a 2002 film by Tunisian writer/director Raja Amari), and I've been a fan of hers ever since. The Israel Film Academy nominated her for a Best Actress award in 2004 (for the role of "Amal" in *The Syrian Bride),* and when she was named Best Actress last year for her performance as "Salma," she became the first Palestinian actress ever accorded this honor (even though *Lemon Tree* was not a commercial success in Israel). Riklis and Arraf wrote the part of "Salma" specifically for Abbass, and it is crafted to reveal all her lights and shadows. She is quite simply one the best film actresses on screen anywhere in the world today, and you will recognize her immediately if you saw the critically acclaimed Indie *The Visitor* (in which she gave a luminous performance as "Mouna").

Ali Suliman ("Ziad") is also an increasingly familiar face in world cinema. Although he had a small role in *The Syrian Bride,* he played one of the lead roles in the Oscar-nominated Palestinian film *Paradise Lost* (2005), and major supporting roles in two recent multiplex films *The Kingdom* and *Body of Lies.* The role of Ziad is a tricky one—he's handsome and charismatic, but haunted by demons. Every woman's nightmare!

Rona Lipaz-Michael, by contrast, is making her screen debut here as "Mira" (although she's had a highly regarded career on the Israeli stage). The counterpoint works beautifully; just as Mira studies Salma and draws inner strength from watching her, so Lipaz-Michael seems to learn her craft right before our eyes by working with Abbass. Although they only meet face-to-face in one brief scene, Riklis and Arraf create a palpable chemistry between Salma and Mira, and their relationship drives the story forward to its bittersweet but emotionally satisfying conclusion.

Doron Tavory ("Israel Navon") is also relatively new, with no major film credits to his name. While he's fine in the part, Riklis and Arraf haven't given Defense Minister Navon much shading, and naming him "Israel" seems out-of-sync with the subtle nuance which characterizes the film as a whole.

Of the three Riklis films I've seen, *Lemon Tree* is his best film to date. (*The Syrian Bride* and *Cup Final,* his critically-acclaimed 1991 film, are both available on DVD). Once again, Riklis proves there are no winners in the Arab/Israeli conflict, only losers. This film is a sincere prayer for peace and the end of enmity between neighbors.

© **Jan Lisa Huttner (4/30/09)—Special for WomenArts**

The Lovely Bones
Directed by Peter Jackson
Screenplay by Philippa Boyens, Fran Walsh, & Peter Jackson
(Based on a novel by Alice Sebold)

Principal Actors: Saoirse Ronan with Stanley Tucci & Mark Wahlberg

The Lovely Bones *is the story of a teenager named Susie who is brutally murdered by an innocuous-looking neighbor. While Mr. Harvey fastidiously covers his tracks, Susie is trapped in a parallel universe called "the Inbetween" (not yet Heaven but no longer Earth), where she watches as her loved ones struggle to go on living without her. Although faithfully based on Alice Sebold's best-selling source novel, the film version of* The Lovely Bones *also gives Susie her own storyline— she has a puzzle she must solve on our behalf before she can enter Heaven (wherever or whatever that might be). With an excellent cast and all the tools of cinema at their command, director Peter Jackson and his team members do an excellent job of finding the core truth in this poignant story, and despite its tragic premise, watching* The Lovely Bones *is an enlivening, enriching and galvanizing experience.*

Penny's Points: ✳✳✳✳½

The Lovely Bones is the story of a teenager named "Susie Salmon" who is lured to a seemingly open (though carefully prepared) location, and then brutally murdered. The perpetrator, "George Harvey," is Susie's neighbor, someone who commits this horrendous act and then continues to live right across the street from her grieving family.

When the police arrive, canvassing the street, Mr. Harvey is respectful and helpful, offering them cookies and blaming himself for not being more observant. ("No, um, no, I don't think I saw anything unusual.") Face-to-face with Susie's devastated father, he offers his condolences, man-to-man. In other words, Mr. Harvey is a monster, but he's so inconspicuous that he embodies nothing less than "the banality of evil."

While Mr. Harvey (Stanley Tucci) fastidiously covers his tracks, Susie (Saoirse Ronan) speaks to us directly from "the Inbetween." Trapped in a parallel universe that's not yet Heaven but also no longer Earth, Susie can only watch as her loved ones struggle to go on living without her. The Inbetween is a literary device, of course, a way to tell a complex story from multiple points of view. There is no Inbetween, and who knows if there's a Heaven, but the basic facts of the narrative are simple enough: Susie is dead and Mr. Harvey is alive.

In Alice Sebold's best-selling source novel, there are three concurrent threads. While Susie watches Mr. Harvey, she also provides updates on her family members (father Jack, mother Abigail, sister Lindsay, brother Buckley, and grandmother Lynn) as well as her boyfriend (Ray Singh). But in the film version of *The Lovely Bones,* screenwriters Philippa Boyens and Fran Walsh have also given Susie her own storyline. She's no longer just an observer of other people's thoughts and deeds; she has a puzzle she must solve, a work she must do on our behalf. For the sake of those who haven't seen *The Lovely Bones* yet, I'm going to be oblique: let's just say that to leave the Inbetween and get to Heaven (wherever or whatever that might be), Susie must relinquish her "birth family" and come to recognize herself as a member of her "death family."

The Salmons live in a comfortable, upscale suburb just outside Philadelphia (where our nation's founders signed our *Declaration of Independence* and wrote our Constitution). They are good people, ordinary "Americans" in the very best sense. "Jack" (Mark Wahlberg) is an accountant and a devoted family man, and his wife "Abigail" (Rachel Weisz), nestled in his warm, loving arms, is a homemaker. Abigail has deliberately stepped back from the more flamboyant excesses of her own mother "Grandma Lynn" (Susan Sarandon), totally dedicating herself to the well-being of her children.

Susie is quite specific about the date of her murder: "I was fourteen when I was murdered on December 6, 1973." Count backwards, and that means Jack and Abigail were both born sometime during the Great Depression, and they were children during World War II. Therefore, creating a safe, nurturing environment is a great accomplishment for them, and they think they've succeeded. Susie, their firstborn, is smart, pretty, and popular; "Lindsay" (Rose McIver) has already been tracked into a "Gifted" program; "Buckley" (Christian Thomas Ashdale), though still just a kid, is playful and affectionate. All three Salmon children are full of promise.

Once they are finally convinced that Susie is gone, however, Jack's malignant guilt eats away at him from the inside, and losing Jack as well as Susie causes Abigail to unravel. When Jack asks Grandma Lynn to come help out, Abigail flees. But even though he's obsessed, hounding the police constantly with meaningless "clues," Jack still manages to go to work every day and bring a paycheck home every week. Lindsey pushes herself athletically (consciously determined to fight back should anyone ever threaten her), while Buckley goes to school and soccer practice, implicitly accepting Grandma Lynn as his new "mother." Slowly the household settles into new routines.

Meanwhile "Ray Singh" (Reece Ritchie), Susie's boyfriend, takes his own painful steps forward. Leaving school for the last time on the day of her murder, Susie is carrying a love note from Ray in her bag, but she only finds out about it when a girl named "Ruth" (Carolyn Dando) finds the letter and gives it back to him. Sensitive and artistic, Ruth feels Susie's continued presence in the Inbetween, and by validating Ray's despair, she helps him to accept it and move on.

With an excellent cast and all the tools of cinema at their command (especially music, sound design, and special visual effects), director Peter Jackson and his team members do an excellent job of finding the core truth in this poignant story: even after she's dead, Susie's world is brighter, more vivid, and more passionate than Mr. Harvey's world can ever be. Even as they grieve, the people in Susie's world continue to share, to love, to bond in new ways, and to grow older, and yes, wiser together. But Mr. Harvey is always alone; once his victim is gone, he has no one and nothing to fill the emptiness inside.

And so, despite its tragic premise, watching *The Lovely Bones* is an enlivening and enriching experience for its audience. Human life, with all its joys and sorrows, is shown to be full of possibility and hope for the future, and Susie's last words are precisely the right words: "I wish you all a long and happy life."

SPOILER ALERT!!!
Please do NOT read until AFTER you have seen *The Lovely Bones!*

Susie is quite specific about the date of her murder: December 6, 1973. "It was still back when people believed things like that didn't happen," Susie says, but that's not quite correct. Everyone knew that women and girls (yes, even women and girls from good homes and good families) were routinely abused, raped, and sometimes even murdered. And everyone knew the perpetrators were often the victim's intimates: fathers, brothers, uncles, neighbors. People knew, they always knew, they just didn't talk about it.

1973. Alice Sebold doesn't tell us why she picked this specific year for this particular story, but I can tell you that the US Supreme Court issued its *Roe v Wade* decision on January 22, 1973, and that's when everything started to change for women, at least in this country. Women in many other countries, countries without our laws and without our freedoms, still suffer in silence. When she first arrives in the Inbetween, Susie thinks she's "a one;" it takes her some time to understand (and accept) that she's actually one of many. Mr. Harvey has killed before and he will kill again, and he is also one of many.

As a novelist, Alice Sebold has no need to make an overtly political point or become personally embroiled in any of the rhetoric of the acrimonious pro-life/pro-choice debate. By telling the story of one life cut short with such skill and grace, Sebold also makes a case for all the girls and all the women whose lives have been brutally impacted by male violence.

Regular readers of my reviews already know that I deliberately avoid all source material before I see a film, even thought this stance sometimes puts me behind a curve in popular culture. I'd certainly heard buzz about Sebold's novel. I knew Oprah had featured *The Lovely Bones* on one of her book club broadcasts, I kinda sorta knew it was narrated by a dead girl, and maybe I had even heard somewhere along the way that Sebold herself had once been raped.

But when I learned for sure that director Peter Jackson and his screenwriting collaborators Philippa Boyens and Fran Walsh planned to do a film adaptation, I did my best to forget all of this. By the time I entered the theater on Tuesday, December 1 to attend a critics screening, I can honestly tell you I had no idea what to expect. Furthermore, I'll also confess that it took me some time to "get it."

After an hour or so, while I was still trying to figure out where the Inbetween was, I became vaguely aware of the fact that the colleague to my left (another woman) was sniffling. I remember wondering if she had a cold. But very soon after that I began to realize that "Holly" (Nikki SooHoo), Susie's friend in the Inbetween, was another victim, and then I started crying, and I knew instantly that my colleague was crying too.

I was supposed to see another film that day, but when *The Lovely Bones* ended, I went into the Ladies Room to wash my face, knowing I was completely spent. I went home, still deeply moved, and the next day I bought the book. Since that time, I have read the book, seen the film three more times, and done the requisite background research on Alice Sebold, her life, and her rape.

It's true: sometime during the winter of her freshman year in college, Alice Sebold was brutally raped. She survived, but later the police told her that another girl had been raped in similar circumstances. The police told Alice she was lucky to be alive; the other girl, they told her, was not so lucky. No, I didn't consciously know any of this the first time I saw *The Lovely Bones,* certainly not in any depth or with any clarity, but by the time I reached the Ladies Room, I felt the full weight of what I had just seen.

Furthermore, having had the luxury of watching the film several times now, I am in awe of its delicate construction. The truth is I really believe this film is even better than its source book. The filmmakers have pared the narrative down to its essential elements, and they have honored all of Sebold's intricate symbolism (for example, it's no accident that Mr. Harvey keeps Susie's remains in a "safe").

But locating Susie in the Inbetween and giving her a "work" she must do before she can get to Heaven helps us understand the importance of her story. Violence against women is horrible in its concrete particulars, but recognizing its truly universal dimensions can be galvanizing.

"When Everything Changed" is actually the title of a new book by *New York Times* columnist Gail Collins:

> "Once young women had confidence that they could make it through training and the early years of their profession without getting pregnant, their attitude toward careers that require a long-term commitment changed. They began applying to medical, law, dental, and business schools in large numbers. This was an enormous shift." (Page 102)

1973 was a milestone year for American women, and women are now active participants in almost every aspect of modern American life. Am I saying that female doctors, female lawyers, and yes, female filmmakers (whose career opportunities followed a similar trajectory) are more inclined than their male counterparts to see violence against women from the victim's perspective? You bet!

If I ruled the world, *The Lovely Bones* would be nominated next week for a Best Adapted Screenplay Oscar, but there is almost no chance that this will happen. Culturally, we're still kinda sorta stuck in the Inbetween. Just like Susie, we have some work to do before we can get to Heaven.

© **Jan Lisa Huttner (1/15/10)—Special for WomenArts**

Marie Antoinette
Written and Directed by Sofia Coppola

Principal Actors: Kirsten Dunst
with Marianne Faithful & Jason Schwartzman

Coppola's narrative is based on Antonia Fraser's sympathetic biography Marie Antoinette: The Journey. *When I read it, after having seen the film a second time, I was surprised to find that the screenplay was remarkably faithful to the historical record. The facts of Marie Antoinette's intimate life are shockingly accessible. I would be delighted to see Ms. Coppola receive Oscar nominations this year in both the "Best Director" and "Best Adapted Screenplay" categories. This time, I really do believe that she has earned them.*

Penny's Points: ✱✱✱✱½

Although I am totally committed to supporting women filmmakers in their fight against the "celluloid ceiling," my emotions were painfully mixed the day Sofia Coppola became the first American woman in Oscar history to receive a "Best Director" nomination. I thought *Lost in Translation* was way over-rated. I suspected that members of the Academy of Motion Picture Arts & Sciences were just trying to make up for past mistakes (as they often do): they gave *Frida* six nominations but didn't nominate director Julie Taymor, so the next year, having taken a lot of flack, they nominated Coppola.

For these reasons, I refused to read any of the hype about *Marie Antoinette* in advance. I went into the screening room determined to see it with fresh eyes and an open mind. Alas, although I doubt it will happen, I would be delighted to see Ms. Coppola receive Oscar nominations this year in both the "Best Director" and "Best Adapted Screenplay" categories. This time, I really do believe that she has earned them.

Coppola's narrative is based on Antonia Fraser's sympathetic biography *Marie Antoinette: The Journey*. When I read it, after having seen the film a second time, I was surprised to find that the screenplay was remarkably faithful to the historical record. The facts of Marie Antoinette's intimate life are shockingly accessible. Letters documenting obsessive interest in her menstrual cycle, for example, are now museum treasurers, displayed side-by-side with articles of clothing, jewelry, furniture, and obscene pamphlets depicting her as a voracious sexual predator. Furthermore, the poor girl, whose designated godparents were the King and Queen of Portugal, was actually born on the day of the great Lisbon earthquake (November 2, 1755). Sometimes truth really is stranger than fiction.

Contrary to many of my fellow film critics, I believe that the opulent mise-en-scene and the provocative soundtrack of *Marie Antoinette* are both subordinate to the narrative rather than ends in themselves. As I see it, Coppola's goal is to depict the arc of a controversial life in such as way as to make that life relevant to viewers who not only lack interest in history but downright scorn it. (Remember, even while this film was under development American congressman were insisting that the "French Fries" served in their dining room be renamed "Freedom Fries.")

Far from being a party animal (count the critics referencing Cyndi Lauper's 1983 chart buster "Girls Just Wanna Have Fun"), Coppola's Marie is the ultimate good girl. Her overriding concern is to make other people happy, and the one person she is most eager to please is her mother, Austrian Empress Maria Theresa. Marie is only fourteen years old when Maria Theresa arranges her marriage to the heir to the French throne, and once Marie leaves Vienna and moves to Versailles, she never sees her mother again.

But Maria Theresa's insistent letters continuously assert her control over her daughter's life, and one of Coppola's master strokes was to cast singer Marianne Faithful in this critical role. Faithful's voice is rich, dark, husky and powerful, and wherever she is, whatever she's doing, this is the voice from which Marie can never escape. Hence her sadness in the midst of revelry; when Marie parties she does it to win the love of sycophants, and when she drinks, she does it to dull the nagging voice that's always in her head.

Maria Theresa has pride of place in the huge crowd of courtiers and hangers-on watching and waiting for this immature young girl and her equally inexperienced consort to mate, as if they were nothing more than domesticated animals with exalted blood lines. Their most intimate acts are sources of endless speculation, advice, and criticism. Even with all her finery, it is impossible to envy Marie Antoinette. Only a fool would want to walk in this woman's fancy shoes for more than the film's 123-minute run time.

And yet, despite all the odds, Marie and Louis do eventually come together as a couple, and by the end they are clearly affectionate friends. When furious revolutionaries descend on Versailles, friends urge Marie to run, but she chooses to remain with Louis. Coppola didn't make any of this up, and she doesn't try to romanticize any of it. Devoted to their royal duty as well as to each other, Marie and Louis stand their ground together as husband and wife as well as the King and Queen of France.

We know from the beginning how it will end. Coppola doesn't need to show Marie walking up to the guillotine. It's enough to know that she's matured from girlhood to womanhood with both her courage and dignity fully intact. Although she is only 24 years old, Kirsten Dunst already has a huge body of work, and yet nothing prepared me for the depth and poignancy she brings to this role. When the Oscar nominations are announced on January 23, 2007, I hope to see Dunst's name on the list of "Best Actress" candidates.

For those of us who are interested in history, for those of us who believe that "those who forget the past are condemned to repeat it," *Marie Antoinette* holds some valuable lessons.

According to Fraser, Marie never said "Let them eat cake." Quite the contrary, she was known for her philanthropy and was considered more generous in this regard than most of her contemporaries. Furthermore, while she did have an extravagant period, it was of relatively short duration. After Maria Therese Charlotte, her first child, was born in 1778, Marie settled into a domestic period centered around her growing family. What pushed the French economy to the breaking point was Louis XVI's financial support for the American Revolution.

Coppola doesn't belabor any of these points, but she does embed them in her narrative. She shows Louis and Marie living in a bubble, much like our current leaders do. To the extent that he paid attention, Louis put the needs of his own people second to besting the British in a game of global hegemony. The consequences were dire. "Let them eat Freedom Fries!"

© **Jan Lisa Huttner (11/01/06)—Special for Digital Filmmaker**

The Namesake
Directed by Mira Nair
Screenplay by Sooni Taraporevala
(Based on a novel by Jhumpa Lahiri)

Principal Actors: Kal Penn with Irrfan Khan & Tabu

The Namesake *is the rare case in which both book and film are equally strong and their differences actually complement each other. With Gogol as her focal point, Lahiri works out into the wider world, whereas Nair focuses on Ashima and Ashoke and works in. In both cases, youthful experiments are counter-pointed with middle-aged accommodations.*

Penny's Points: ✳✳✳✳½

Mira Nair burst onto the international film scene in 1988, the year her first feature film, *Salaam Bombay!* was released. The applause was deafening. *Bombay* won five awards, including the prestigious Golden Camera award from the Cannes Film Festival jury. The folks giving out BAFTA, Cesar, and Golden Globe awards all nominated it for "Best Foreign Language Film," and then it received the ultimate honor: an Oscar nomination.

Heady stuff, and after *Bombay,* Nair (rhymes with "fire") made seven more feature films (including two for American cable television) racking up an almost uncountable number of nominations from critics, guilds, and audiences alike. Having seen them all, and loved them all, I can say without reservation that *The Namesake* is Mira Nair's best film to date. Jhumpa Lahiri's best-selling novel is the perfect vehicle for Nair, allowing her to explore with exquisite intensity the two themes that have most marked her career: the lessons to be learned from arranged marriages now that Hollywood has commercialized romantic love; and the search for "home" in an ever-flattening world.

Lahiri's novel (also called *The Namesake*) is the story of Gogol Ganguli. Gogol enters the world on the first page, and he's alone with his thoughts on the last page. Gogol is an East Coast kid: born in a Cambridge, Massachusetts hospital, he's raised in a Boston suburb, and heads one state south to Yale University in his teens before settling into professional life in Manhattan, one state further south, as a young adult. Although Ashima Bhaduri and Ashoke Ganguli, Gogol's mother and father, are essential characters, the novel is equally concerned with Gogol's romantic coming-of-age: his first infatuation (with Ruth), his first committed relationship (with Maxine), his first casual affair (with Bridget), and his first marriage (to Moushumi). He's a type Lahiri presumably knows very well: a self-described ABCD or "American-Born Confused Deshi." (Although she was born in London, Lahiri grew up in Rhode Island.) It's the brilliant work of a talented young woman just entering full adulthood. (Lahiri married in 2001 and her first child was born in 2002.)

Nair's film, by contrast, is the work of a mature woman, twice-married and the mother of a teenager. She's embedded Gogol's story within a Ganguli family saga: Ashoke now opens the narrative and Ashima closes it. Since it's no longer told in flashback, the details of their arranged marriage have more immediacy, and we get to know them as they are getting to know each other. Their early years in America are filled with longing for India, and their days and nights are punctuated with phone calls from and visits to Calcutta. Bundled up against a cold their relatives will never fully appreciate, they send letters and pictures "home," until, eventually, as year follows year "home" becomes their house on Pemberton Road.

Sophisticated film lovers no longer insist that an adaptation be completely faithful to its source. We now recognize that sometimes the film is actually better. (*The Devil Wears Prada* is a recent example.) *The Namesake* is the rare case in which both book and film are equally strong and their differences actually complement each other. With Gogol as her focal point, Lahiri works out into the wider world, whereas Nair focuses on Ashima and Ashoke and works in. In both cases, youthful experiments are counter-pointed with middle-aged accommodations.

The voice of the novelist and the eye of the filmmaker are in perfect synergy. In scene after scene, Nair creates iconic images that depict intense emotions. Facial expressions, subtle gestures, even pieces of furniture, all capture the ineffable. Before they've ever made eye contact, Ashima sees Ashoke's shoes, and the tiny moment in which she daringly slips her feet into them resonates throughout the entire film. Yes, the novelist has described these shoes in detail, but it is the filmmaker who shows us how well they fit. They're big, of course, but not too big. These shoes, on Ashoke's feet, will take Ashima to America, and she immediately senses that they will protect her without overwhelming her.

The casting is also perfect: "Ashima" (Tabu) is a luminous beauty whereas "Ashoke" (Irrfan Khan) is a sweet-faced geek. Kal Penn, current filming the sequel to his highly-successful 2004 feature *Harold & Kumar Go to White Castle,* brings a comic touch to his performance as Gogol that helps the filmmaker age him from 15 to 30. Jacinda Barrett, who played a similar role to great effect in *The Human Stain,* is lovely as "Max", and Zuleikha Robinson, alluring in *Hidalgo,* is ravishing here as "Moushumi."

DP Frederick Elmes' cinematography is also outstanding. Well-known in the Indie world for his work with Jim Jarmusch (*Broken Flowers, Coffee and Cigarettes, Mystery Train,* and *Night on Earth*) and David Lynch (*Eraserhead, Blue Velvet,* and *Wild at Heart*), Elmes here incorporates elements from time spent in both Bill Condon's academia (*Kinsey*) and Ang Lee's suburbia (*The Ice Storm*). His palette deftly differentiates the past (with its golden memories and blood-tinged nightmares) from the present (with its lonely moments and communal rites of passage). Nair and Elmes even give us a tour of the inner arches of the Taj Mahal, finding intimate angles just as beautiful as the grand picture postcard entrance.

For over forty years, male critics have described the musical *Fiddler on the Roof* as "sentimental," always assuming that *Fiddler* was primarily targeted at Jews pining for Anatevka; but Jews are not the world's only exiles. Audiences everywhere have embraced *Fiddler* (where it was as popular in Japan as it was in Israel). Like the *Fiddler* team, Nair and screenwriter Sooni Taraporevala are eloquent students of Diaspora. Just as Tevye, the father figure in *Fiddler,* is expelled from Anatevka, Jay, the father figure played by Roshan Seth in Nair's 1991 film *Mississippi Masala,* is expelled from Uganda. But Ashima is like Tevye's daughter Hodel; she makes a conscious choice when she leaves Calcutta. The dilemma first articulated in the lyrics Sheldon Harnick wrote for Hodel ("Far From the Home I Love") has now achieved its poignant realization in *The Namesake.*

Invocations of the goddess Saraswati open and close Nair's film, reminding us that human life is both eternal and evanescent: home is a place we hold sacred in our hearts, but it is also the place where we put on our shoes each morning to greet the new day.

© Jan Lisa Huttner (3/1/07)—Special for Digital Filmmaker

Please Give
Written & Directed by Nicole Holofcener

Principal Actors: Catherine Keener
with Ann Guilbert & Rebecca Hall

"Kate" (Catherine Keener) lives in a cramped Manhattan apartment and owns a resale shop specializing in vintage furniture. She's been comfortable in her own skin for years, but as Please Give *opens, something's bugging her, and that*

something is her 90-year-old neighbor "Andra" (Ann Guilbert). The smell of death is suddenly permeating her home as well as her business, and Kate is spooked.

"Liberal Guilt" is an easy target for a comedy writer. Holofcener has a great time making us laugh at Kate's expense, and Keener, as the film's anchor, gracefully plays the butt of every joke. A woman like Kate will always fall short of her own ideal, but what's the alternative? The clocks just keep ticking, and in Holofcener's world, giving up is far worse than failing.

Holofcener's three prior films all had wonderful moments, but this time the whole really is greater than the sum of its parts. Brava!

Penny's Points: ✳✳✳✳½

Please Give is a spring flower. When I left the screening room, I carried it with me like a bud, and for two days now I've watched it unfurl. This is the first Nicole Holofcener film to make me feel so enraptured. Going into *Walking and Talking, Lovely & Amazing,* and *Friends with Money,* I'd hoped for the best, but left disappointed. For sure all three of Holofcener's prior films had wonderful moments, but none of them quite came together for me. This time, though, the whole really is greater than the sum of its parts.

"Kate" (Catherine Keener) and her husband "Alex" (Oliver Platt) live in a cramped Manhattan apartment with their daughter "Abby" (Sarah Steele), and while they're certainly comfortable, they're definitely not wealthy people. In fact, in New York terms, they're practically paupers. Middle-aged and middle-class, Kate and Alex are also middlemen—they own a resale shop specializing in vintage furniture, and their stock comes primarily from estate sales.

"Vintage," "estate sale," these are nice words, but the reality is that Kate and Alex spend most of their time sorting through the personal possessions of the recently deceased. Once upon a time, people treasured items handed down to them by loved ones: Mama's table, Papa's chair. But these days most of us would rather buy our own "stuff," and when people die we call in experts (like Kate and Alex) to price their residue and cart it away.

First Kate comforts the bereaved, then she watches competitors cherry-pick her booty. She's been doing this job for years, and she knows she's only one part of a long merchandise chain. Her good taste is matched by a solid reputation, and she has no illusions. But as the film opens, something's bugging Kate, and that something is her 90 year old neighbor "Andra" (Ann Guilbert). The smell of death is suddenly permeating Kate's home as well as her business, and she's spooked.

Andra's primary caregiver, her granddaughter "Rebecca" (Rebecca Hall), is a young woman in her late 20s with the patience of a saint. Every day, Rebecca arrives with groceries, walks the dog, and does everything she can to be helpful and cheerful as Andra's world shrinks down to the confines of her apartment. Kate and Rebecca have been passing each other in the hallway for years, and Rebecca knows that Kate and Alex have already purchased Andra's apartment. So rather than face her own concerns about Andra's failing health, Rebecca stews about Kate, mentally accusing her of measuring out the minutes of Andra's remaining time on earth.

Rebecca's not wrong. When the time comes to knock down the adjoining wall, combining the two apartments will have obvious benefits (especially for teenage Abby in her "ugly duckling" phase). But Kate isn't doing anything to hasten Andra's journey, in fact money from the sale is probably making it possible for Andra to stay put. Nevertheless, to assuage her guilty conscience, Kate decides to have a party, inviting both of Andra's granddaughters—moon-faced Rebecca as well as her spiky sister "Mary" (Amanda Peet).

Ann Guilbert is a hoot as the irascible Andra, a feisty crone determined to live life on her own terms for as long as possible. She may depend on Rebecca, but it's Mary, someone with her own sharp tongue, who is her favorite sparring partner. Watching her grandmother and her sister go at it, Rebecca Hall responds like a floppy-eared dog caught between two tigresses. She's much too sincere to get a word in edgewise, and Hall's body language makes it clear that she stopped trying years ago.

Amanda Peet bites into Mary's sarcastic dialogue, gleefully seducing Sarah Steele's eager Abby (who thinks Mary is the cat's meow), and slyly flirting with Oliver Platt's bemused Alex (even though he knows Kate is watching). Keener, as the film's anchor, turns Kate into a classic "straight man," gracefully playing the butt of every joke. The party scene is a comic gem, with every member of the ensemble rising to the occasion.

Holofcener's multidimensional characters are all true to a very specific milieu, but the emotions swirling inside them are universal and deeply resonant. It's autumn in New York, and everyone's chattering about the leaves. After the party, Rebecca gives in to the hype and takes Andra out for a drive in the country. Unexpectedly moved by the wild burst of color, Rebecca finally resigns herself to Andra's inevitable death, even as Andra, standing right beside her, just keeps kvetching. You don't have to live in Manhattan to appreciate the poignancy of this scene.

Meanwhile Kate is fretting about a vase, also painted in fall colors of red and gold. She bought it from man who was eager to unload his dead mother's "junk" as quickly as possible, but the vase has turned out to be surprisingly valuable. Kate's in a quandary, so she decides to return it. The man thanks her, takes the vase, and politely shuts his door. Close up on Kate as we hear the sound of vase hitting wall.

"Liberal Guilt" is an easy target for a comedy writer, and Holofcener has a great time making us laugh at Kate's expense. Try as she might, Kate cannot save the world. Her daughter Abby's complexion and body type are as fixed and immutable as the hunger and poverty outside their front door. So why try? Because Holofcener genuinely believes that giving up is far worse than failing. If Kate stopped trying, then *Please Give* would be a tragedy.

It's hard to be a "good person" in this screwed up modern world of ours. A woman like Kate will always fall short of her own ideal. Alas, there is no alternative—the clocks just keep ticking. *Please Give* is a wise and witty new variation on an old Borscht Belt punch line: "The food is awful and the portions are so small!"

© **Jan Lisa Huttner (5/5/10) Special for WomenArts**

The Prize Winner of Defiance, Ohio
Written & Directed by Jane Anderson
(Based on a memoir by Terry Ryan)

Principal Actors: Julianne Moore
with Woody Harrelson & Laura Dern

Filmmaker Jane Anderson (who won Emmy and WGA awards in 1993 for The Positively True Adventures of the Alleged Texas Cheerleader-Murdering Mom, *and received Emmy, WGA, and DGA nominations in 2003 for* Normal*), takes her lead from Tuff, adopting Tuff's triumphant tone as her own. Evelyn never gave in to the sorrows of her life, and Anderson understands that her job is to prove that Evelyn did, in fact, manage to keep it all together. Moore gives a performance of incredible depth and nuance: smiling on the outside, screaming on the inside.*

Penny's Points: ✶✶✶✶½

"You know it's a bad year for women when none of the best picture nominees even features one in a lead performance," wrote *Los Angeles Times* staff writer Rachel Abramowitz on February 1st, one day after the Academy of Motion Picture Arts and Sciences (AMPAS) released this year's list of Oscar contenders. And Abramowitz is not alone; many women are questioning this year's selections. But if all this is news to you, you may well ask an obvious question: what's missing?

If I ruled the world, this year's list of Best Pictures would include *King Kong* and *The Prize Winner of Defiance, Ohio,* two films driven by powerhouse performances by A-list actresses in parts specifically tailored for them by popular female screenwriters. Both Naomi Watts (the star of *King Kong*) and Julianne Moore (the star of *Prize Winner*) were so compelling that I'm having a hard time choosing between them in my parallel universe, so I'm incensed about the fact that I don't get the chance to root for either one of them here on planet Earth. But at least Naomi Watts was in *King Kong,* so AMPAS be damned, lots of people saw her great work. Julianne Moore, however, starred in *Prize Winner,* which opened on a paltry 41 screens on the last Friday of September, and grossed a mere $626,310 before it was pulled from commercial release eight weeks later (by which time it was down to 15 screens).

Prize Winner is based on Terry ("Tuff") Ryan's best-selling 2001 memoir *The Prize Winner of Defiance, Ohio: How My Mother Raised 10 Kids on 25 Words or Less.* It's an Eisenhower-era haunted house movie in which the monsters are bankers, milkmen, priests, and policemen, while the damsel-in-distress is a tenacious Catholic housewife. Evelyn Lehman was a budding young journalist when she met and married Leo ("Kelly") Ryan in 1936, and like so many talented women of her generation, she put aside career ambitions and devoted herself to raising a family. But Kelly turned cruel under the weight of his responsibilities, and when he started drinking away his paycheck every night, Evelyn needed for a way to make her verbal skills profitable. She turned contesting into a family sport, and became one of the biggest money-makers of the '50s.

This could have been grim stuff, but filmmaker Jane Anderson (who won Emmy and WGA awards in 1993 for *The Positively True Adventures of the Alleged Texas Cheerleader-Murdering Mom,* and received Emmy, WGA, and DGA nominations in 2003 for *Normal),* takes her lead from Tuff, adopting Tuff's triumphant tone as her own. Evelyn never gave in to the sorrows of her life, and Anderson understands that her job is to prove that Evelyn did, in fact, manage to keep it all together.

Moore gives a performance of incredible depth and nuance: smiling on the outside, screaming on the inside. She is always acting the part of the perfect Mom for her brood, fearful that Kelly's bitterness will infect her children like a virus and ruin their lives. Almost every scene takes place in the Ryan's cramped and cacophonous little two-story house, but Anderson fills each frame with so much color and light that the viewer is torn in two: on the one hand, it feels like it would be fun to live there, but on the other hand, it's downright claustrophobic. Evelyn is only allowed one extended escape scene; when Tuff, one of the middle children, gets her driver's license, she takes Evelyn to a meeting of the Affadaisies (a club for fellow contesters), but their one-day excursion carries a high price.

How does Evelyn do it? She thinks like a baseball player. Every new contest is another chance at bat. Sometimes she hits a home run, sometimes she hits a single, sometimes she strikes out, but her lifetime average is phenomenal. (The sights and sounds of baseball are ever-present in the film. Kelly is a fanatical Cleveland Indians fan, and two of their sons make steady progress from Little League up to minor league careers, while the family assembles to cheer them on through every game.)

The role of Kelly Ryan must have seemed pretty thankless on paper, nevertheless Woody Harrelson succeeds in giving the man a soul. Even though he loves his wife, her success humiliates him. The whole town knows that all their money comes from Evelyn's winnings, and the guys at work hound him mercilessly. So it's clear that Kelly is just as much a victim of societal expectations as Evelyn is, and he's never portrayed as a one-dimensional villain.

Laura Dern also has a small but spicy role as Dortha Schaefer, the leader of the Affadaisies. Although Dortha and Evelyn rarely see each other face-to-face, they are both lively letter writers, and Anderson uses their correspondence to propel Evelyn out into the wide-world beyond her house. However physically constrained she may be, Evelyn is a voracious mental traveler.

I frankly don't know why this film didn't do better at box office, and I predict it will be very popular when it hits the DVD shelves on March 14th. It will, of course, be categorized as "a chick flick," and many men will therefore be loath to see it. That's a shame, because Evelyn Ryan was as uniquely American as Truman Capote, Edward R. Morrow and her other well-known male contemporaries, and even though she encased herself in girdles and dowdy dresses, the heroic dimensions of "a life well lived" are clear for all to see.

© **Jan Lisa Huttner (2/28/06)—Special for Digital Filmmaker**

The Producers
Directed by Susan Stroman
Written by Mel Brooks & Thomas Meehan

Principal Actors: Nathan Lane
with Matthew Broderick & Uma Thurman

If you just don't like musicals, and many people don't, then none of this matters, but if you do, then there's no contest: the musical version of The Producers *(2005) is much funnier than the original and, despite its length, it moves at a much brisker pace. When I saw the stage version, I laughed my head off. When I saw the screen version, I laughed even harder. All the tiny little details, the things no one sitting in front of the proscenium can really see, kept me in stitches: the poster of "King Leer" in Max's office, the animatronic birds wearing swastikas, the Iron Cross medals adorning Ulla's tits, all hilarious. How great to see Leo visualizing the dancers in his dream sequence as "beautiful girls wearing nothing but pearls." And watching Roger play Hitler, so desperate for affirmation, you can understand why the audience is seduced.*

Penny's Points: ✳✳✳✳✳½

Screening rooms are a lot like libraries: silence reigns supreme. Most critics don't need anyone to shush them; they're kept in check by peer pressure, and part of the game is to stifle your reactions so no one knows what you're thinking. But the night I saw *The Producers (2005)* early last December, the crowd was doubled over with laughter. So imagine my surprise when I started reading all the negative reviews…

The Producers holds a prestigious Broadway record: it won 12 Tony awards in 2001, taking the prize in every possible category in which it was a contender. Nevertheless domestic box office grosses for the film adaptation were dismal. So far, the film has recouped less than half of its $45 million production budget. Four Golden Globe nominations failed to produce a single Oscar nomination. What went wrong?

The first version of *The Producers (1968)* was an 88-minute farce made for under $1 million. The screenplay, the first of the eleven he's seen filmed, won Mel Brooks his only Oscar to date ("Best Screenplay Written Directly for the Screen") in 1969. By contrast, both the 2001 Broadway stage version of *The Producers* and the 2005 film version are elaborately staged musicals. Although most of the basic plot points remain constant, the storytelling formats are completely incommensurate.

For the sake of the uninitiated, here's an overview:

One fine day, Manhattan accounting firm Whitehall & Marks dispatches nebbishy "Leo Bloom" to audit the books of washed-up impresario "Max Bialystock." While quizzing Max about a minor discrepancy, Leo makes a starting discovery: "You can make more money with a flop than with a hit." Exhausted by his recent string of failures, Max seizes on this "cockamamie scheme," convincing Leo they can bilk the IRS and escape to Rio de Janeiro. Working together, they diligently scrape the bottom of every talent barrel, but instead of failure the result is a smashing success. Their musical extravaganza *Springtime for Hitler: A Gay Romp with Adolph and Eva in the Bergesgarten* is so over-the-top, it's irresistible. Convicted of fraud and sent to Sing Sing, Max and Leo immediately start selling shares in a new production to their fellow prisoners.

The success of the original was built on two critical factors: star power and deliberate bad taste. When Brooks cast Zero Mostel as Max, he was Broadway's miracle man. The original production of *Fiddler on the Roof,* which opened in 1964, was supposed to be a box office failure ("too ethnic"), but with Mostel playing the central part of "Teyve," it became a box office giant. *Fiddler* made yiddishkeit respectable, enabling Jewish audiences to publicly mourn the shtetls destroyed in the Holocaust, while good-hearted people everywhere empathized. The move from sentimentality to transgressive comedy was made possible by the "Six Day War" in 1967. Like their ancient king David facing off against Goliath, the people of Israel had scored an amazing victory against the combined Arab armies. Jews had proven themselves as warriors, so who better than "Tevye" to "dance on Hitler's grave," and thereby embody the aphorism "He who laughs last, laughs best!"

Of course, most people didn't get it, and many Jews who had personal memories of World War II were deeply offended by Brooks' determination to treat Hitler as a subject for comedy. But over the years, the cult status of *The Producers (1968)* grew, and thirty years later, a movie about the making of a Broadway musical was reclaimed as a Broadway musical. Laugh lines in the original were transformed into melodies. Aesthetic elements evolved from cheap kitsch into deliriously extravagant costumes and props. Supporting players like "Ulla" (the secretary) and "Fritz" (the playwright) became fully-drawn characters, and, best of all, Brooks jiggered the plot so that "Roger De Bris" (the director) could move from back stage to center stage in order to personally take on the role of Hitler on Opening Night.

If you just don't like musicals, and many people don't, then none of this matters, but if you do, then there's no contest: the musical version of *The Producers (2005)* is much funnier than the original and, despite its length, it moves at a much brisker pace. When I saw the stage version, I laughed my head off. When I saw the screen version, I laughed even harder. All the tiny little details, the things no one sitting in front of the proscenium can really see, kept me in stitches: the poster of "King Leer" in Max's office, the animatronic birds wearing swastikas, the Iron Cross medals adorning Ulla's tits, all hilarious. How great to see Leo visualizing the dancers in his dream sequence as "beautiful girls wearing nothing but pearls." And watching Roger play Hitler, so desperate for affirmation, you can understand why the audience is seduced.

But there's a worm in the apple that even I couldn't ignore: Matthew Broderick. Broderick is best-known for his starring

role in the John Hughes 1986 comedy *Ferris Bueller's Day Off.*
That was twenty years ago, and the years have finally caught up
with him. Film audiences don't really care about the acclaim his
performance generated on Broadway; we simply reject him as
Leo, the same way we now reject Omar Sharif in *Funny Girl* and
Natalie Wood in *West Side Story.*

The part of Leo Bloom was created by Gene Wilder in his first
major movie role (preceded only by a small but memorable
scene in *Bonnie and Clyde).* The opening credits leave no doubt
that the star of *The Producers (1968)* is Zero Mostel, but their
onscreen chemistry is magic. Their faces are perfect
complements: Mostel's is huge, decrepit, and vaguely deranged;
Wilder's is tiny, soft, and childish. When their faces share the
same frame, Leo's wide-eyed terror is perfectly understandable.

Alas, whatever chemistry Broderick's Leo had with Nathan
Lane's Max on stage, the camera destroyed it. Their joint close-
ups are a disaster, silently eating away at the visual reality of the
Max/Leo relationship, and thereby undermining the whole film.

Luckily Broderick is a talented song-and-dance man with a
warm comic persona, so once he and Lane leave Max's office
and begin interacting with the other characters, Broderick is
fine. He holds his own with Uma Thurman as Ulla, Jon Lovitz
as Mr. Marks, and Will Ferrell as Fritz, and he's at his best when
surrounded by his beautiful girls in pearls.

Nathan Lane, on the other hand, is a joy in every scene,
including the ones rescued for the DVD. Adapting their film
from stage to screen, Brooks and his co-writer Tom Meehan
decided to follow the lead of *Chicago,* eliminating some of Max's
scenes and embellishing some of Leo's. (The film version of
Chicago turned Velma from Roxie's co-star into a supporting
player in her fantasy life.) Brooks assumed his theatre audiences
would enjoy Broadway references – like the African-American
accountant singing "Oh, I debits in the morning and I credits in

the evening, until these ledgers be done" in homage to Paul Robson's timeless rendition of *Old Man River* from *Show Boat* – but uninitiated movie audiences could probably care less. The big number Lane loses comes right at the beginning of the stage version. *I Used to be the King* not only introduces Max's back story, it also exorcises the ghost of Zero Mostel, playing havoc by inverting Tevye's lyrics in *If I Were a Rich Man*. It's now the first and the best of the DVD's deleted scenes.

The DVD also contains a featurette unpacking *I Want to be a Producer,* Leo's biggest number. Like *Chicago*, *The Producers (2005)* benefits greatly from the collaborative efforts of expert lighting designers Peggy Eisenhauer and Jules Fisher.

In the end, though, it's all about Hitler, perfectly played here by Gary Beach (recreating the role which brought him Tony and Drama Desk awards in 2001). Mel Brooks clearly believes that Hitler was history's greatest buffoon. He promised his people a "thousand year Reich," but delivered barely a decade. However horrible his legacy (for Jews, for Russians, for Poles, etc, etc), he did his greatest damage to Germany. The people who believed in him, the people who voted for him, paid a very dear price for his brand of infotainment. Who is the real monster here? Is it the leader or the audience members egging him on? That's the bitter after-taste to this superior confection.

© **Jan Lisa Huttner (06/01/06) —Special for Digital Filmmaker**

Rosenstrasse
Directed by Margarethe von Trotta
Written by von Trotta & Pamela Katz

Principal Actors: Katja Riemann
with Maria Schrader & Svea Lohde

Rosenstrasse is a Holocaust drama directed by a left-wing German feminist that focuses on ordinary people caught in the maelstrom of history. Contemporary framing story about a Manhattan Jewish family works to emphasize shades of gray in a story typically told in b&w. Bottom line: German people did know what was happening. Some protested. Most didn't.

Penny's Points: ✳✳✳✳½

In the United States we are inundated with stories about the Holocaust, from Oscar-winners like *The Pianist* to routine episodes of *Law & Order*. Not so Germany, where the subject still triggers painful debates about guilt and complicity. Now *Rosentrasse*, the new film by acclaimed director Margarethe von Trotta, tells a story almost no one has heard of, just when we were beginning to think we'd heard them all.

Margarethe von Trotta achieved international fame in the late 60s as the star of films by Rainer Werner Fassbinder and Volker Schlondorff, then established herself as one of Europe's most respected woman directors. Her protagonists are typically women forced into active protest by historical circumstance. So von Trotta occupies a unique position; she is an activist, a feminist, and a German intellectual, born in Berlin in 1942 and raised in heart of Hell itself. We have never seen the Holocaust from this point of view before.

The character at the center of *Rosenstrasse* is a young New Yorker from a prosperous Jewish family named Hannah. Her father has just died, and she reaches out to her mother Ruth for comfort, but Ruth withdraws into herself. A woman tries to speak with Ruth at the Shiva, but Ruth rejects her. Hannah hardly knows this cousin, but appeals to her anyway for an explanation of her mother's behavior. Ruth's cousin asks Hannah if she knows anything about a German woman named Lena. No, she does not. But Hannah becomes convinced that only knowledge of Ruth's childhood will bring her mother back to her, and so she flies to Berlin in search of answers.

When Hannah finds her, Lena is ninety years old and still living in Berlin. Hannah does not reveal her identity, she simply tells Lena she's a journalist researching the Holocaust, and pulls out her tape recorder. Lena, alone in her little apartment, is happy to oblige. In her mind's eye, Lena returns to 1943. She is young and beautiful, an Aryan woman deeply in love with her Jewish husband, Fabian Fisher. Over several days of increasing intimacy, Lena tells Hannah her whole story.

When Fabian suddenly disappears, Lena tracks him to the Rosenstrasse, a side street in central Berlin that houses a Jewish social service office. Even though the Jewish spouses of German citizens are supposed to be exempt from deportation, a rumor quickly passes from family to family — their missing relatives are being detained in the Rosenstrasse building. And so, day-by-day, the number of people congregating on the Rosenstrasse grows. Lena takes pity on a young girl named Ruth whose mother has also been arrested. Only eight-years-old with nowhere else to go, Ruth, like her Biblical namesake, cleaves to Lena, goes where she goes, moves in with her.

Rosenstrasse is based on the book *Resistance of the Heart: Intermarriage and the Rosenstrasse Protest in Nazi Germany* by Nathan Stolzfus, a Harvard-trained historian who currently teaches 20th Century European History at Florida State University in Tallahassee. While von Trotta has undoubtedly taken dramatic liberties in filming this story, Stolzfus's sources include women with histories very similar to Lena's and Ruth's. Jewish spouses were interned by the Nazis, and were eventually freed after their German relatives staged a public protest.

This description of the Holocaust is a real departure from the familiar German disavowal of either knowledge or responsibility. On the one hand, no one in *Rosenstrasse* pretends that deportation is anything other than a death sentence. On the other hand, the principal characters, the women who gather on the street, all know that they are German citizens and therefore feel entitled to protest. Lena comes from a prominent family and her brother, recently returned from Stalingrad, is a Wehrmacht officer. Their connections, combined with her aristocratic beauty and his battle wounds, enable them to plead their case directly to Joseph Goebbels (Hitler's Minister of Propaganda). While the actual party scene at which this climactic encounter occurs may be artistic license, the historical record affirms the fact that Goebbels ordered the release of the prisoners because he was afraid of the power of public protest.

Von Trotta clearly wants the German people to face up to their complicity once and for all, to stop saying "We didn't know," or "There was nothing we could do." Most people did know what was happening and could have protested if they had wanted to. (In *Amen*, released in 2002 and now available on DVD, director Costa-Gavras makes the same point. When "good German citizens" learned that their mentally handicapped relatives were targets, they protested and the euthanasia stopped.)

Given the recent rise in anti-Semitism, this is an important message for Europeans to hear. Whatever their objections to the State of Israel, Europeans cannot pretend that once the scourge of Nazism was defeated, Jewish survivors could simply have "returned home" to their otherwise friendly neighbors in Germany, Poland, and elsewhere (the despicable message of both *Nowhere in Africa* and *The Pianist*). There are good reasons why the majority of survivors chose to leave Europe and build new lives for themselves, for the most part in Israel.

But what is the message for Americans? In *Rosenstrasse*, Ruth moves to the United States after the war because that's where her relatives are. She represses her early life and becomes a successful American wife and mother — until her husband's death causes her to feel deserted once again by someone she's loved and trusted. But does this make Ruth just "a victim"? If Lena is a lonely old woman when Hannah finds her, isn't Ruth herself also guilty of abandoning Lena? Of course as a child,

Ruth could do nothing. But if Ruth continues to act out the grievances of a child long after she's become an adult, is she acting responsibly in her new life?

The painful facts of the Holocaust have caused many Jewish Americans to nurse feelings of victimization. *Rosenstrasse* is an opportunity to see shades of gray in many things we thought were black and white.

© **Jan Lisa Huttner (9/01/04)—Special for World Jewish Digest**

Shut Up & *Sing*
Documentary by Barbara Kopple & Cecilia Peck

Key Participants: Natalie Maines
with Emily Robison & Martie Maguire

The great accomplishment of Shut Up & Sing *is to expand our notion of courage, and define new ways in which women can be genuinely courageous. Despite what this year's Oscar candidates* The Departed *and* Letters from Iwo Jima *would have you believe, genuine courage requires more than carrying a gun. For Maines, courage means refusing to back down after saying something she believed, even though she apparently neither planned her remark nor anticipated the onslaught. For Maguire and Robison, courage means facing the outrage of friends and fans, and believing in the future of their group as well as its past.*

Penny's Points: ✱✱✱✱½

Full Disclosure: I hate country music. I once did a long project in Amarillo, Texas and the radio options (or lack thereof) made me nuts. But I knew I had great respect for two-time Oscar-winning documentary film director Barbara Kopple, so when I saw her new film about *The Dixie Chicks* on my Chicago International Film Festival schedule last September, I immediately ordered tickets.

I've now seen *Shut Up & Sing* three times, and the more I know, the better it gets. This is by design. Kopple and her co-director Cecilia Peck set themselves a difficult task: they wanted to make a film that would satisfy the thousands (and probably millions of people) who have been and continue to be consistent fans, but they also wanted their film to appeal to those of us with no knowledge of, or even interest in, the "controversy."

In brief, here's what happened: Martie Maguire, Natalie Maines, and Emily Robison *(The Dixie Chicks)* were at the peak of success (with multiple Grammy awards, platinum & diamond record sales, and highly successful worldwide tours) when they arrived in London to kick-off their "Top of the World Tour" on March 10, 2003. The invasion of Iraq was imminent and protesters were marching in London (and in many other cities as well).

Buoyed by the spirited crowd and apprehensive on her own account as a mother, Maines, the lead singer, made a spontaneous remark that echoed all around the world: "Just so you know, we're ashamed the President of the United States is from Texas." By the time the invasion began ten days later, the Dixie Chicks were considered traitors by a large portion of their historic fan base and blacklisted by the radio stations most responsible for their continued revenue stream.

Kopple and Peck were not formally on board at this point, although they had connected with the group prior to the tour. But as ripples from Maines offhand remark spread though the media, interest in having their story told by a filmmaker of Kopple's stature grew, and Kopple and Peck were given access to all the footage shot in London and immediately afterwards. Kopple and Peck then brought their own team into the mix, filming Maguire, Maines, and Robison as they took tentative next steps which eventually lead to the creation of a whole new professional identity.

The main arc of the story is spread over three years, but Kopple and Peck choose to tell it as a spiral rather than a straight line. The film keeps circling around critical events, so that at each point the viewer knows more than before and therefore has more understanding of what's really at stake. "Fly on the wall" scenes capture intimate moments which are juxtaposed with "talking head" interviews and frenetic concert scenes. Watching *Shut Up & Sing* the third time, I was frankly amazed by how much detail Kopple and Peck were able to capture in the brief 93 minute runtime. I now feel I really understand why Maines' remark triggered such a huge outcry, and why this event became the catalyst for artistic transformation.

Ultimately the great accomplishment of *Shut Up & Sing* is to expand our notion of courage, and define new ways in which women can be genuinely courageous. Despite what this year's Oscar candidates *The Departed* and *Letters from Iwo Jima* would have you believe, genuine courage requires more than carrying a gun. For Maines, courage means refusing to back down after saying something she believed, even though she apparently neither planned her remark nor anticipated the onslaught. For Maguire and Robison, courage means facing the outrage of friends and fans, and believing in the future of their group as well as its past.

There's one sequence that mesmerized me the first time, and it grows more intense every time I see it: *The Dixie Chicks* are in Dallas getting ready to perform in the face of death threats. But this is Dallas, and they know and everyone knows, that someone in this town once had the determination to shoot a president, so no matter how much police protection they have, no, they do not feel safe. Nevertheless, they get ready and they go on stage and they do their show. John F. Kennedy, the author of *Profiles in Courage,* was watching over them that night, and I know he was impressed.

© **Jan Lisa Huttner (1/31/07)—Special for Digital Filmmaker**

Slumdog Millionaire
Directed By Danny Boyle
Co-Directed by Loveleen Tandan
Screenplay by Simon Beaufoy
(Based on a novel by Vikas Swarup)

Principal Actors: Dev Patel
with Ayush Mahesh Khedekar & Tanay Hemant Chheda

Slumdog Millionaire *is the first great film of the new "flat world." "Jamal" (Dev Patel), the hero of* Slumdog Millionaire, *is a Mumbai teenager who becomes a contestant on the Indian version of the TV game show* Who Wants to be a Millionaire. *The plot is as simple as can be: every time* Millionaire's *host asks a new question, Jamal has a flashback. Each flashback leads Jamal to an answer & gives us another chapter of his life story.* Slumdog Millionaire *rests on the shoulders of the nine young actors who play Jamal and his two fellow "musketeers" at various ages, and co-directors Danny Boyle and Loveleen Tandan do a dazzling job of completely individuating them through a complicated series of often heart-breaking adventures. Stay for the credits—they're the icing on the cake. Bravi!*

Penny's Points: ✳✳✳✳½

Slumdog Millionaire is the first great film of the new "Flat World." Using state-of-the-art tools and techniques from "the First World," *Slumdog Millionaire* tells a "Third World" story that respects the difficult lives of its characters while still providing audiences everywhere with a credibly upbeat ending.

"Jamal" (Dev Patel), the hero of *Slumdog Millionaire,* is a teenager who serves tea in a Mumbai call center. Jamal has a dream; he wants to be a contestant on the Indian version of the TV game show *Who Wants to be a Millionaire*—and his dream comes true. Unlikely? Yes. Impossible? No. Reality shows are immensely popular all around the world, and they depend on the emotional investment of audiences who want to watch people like themselves literally transformed into televised "players."

The plot is as simple as can be: every time *Millionaire's* host "Prem" (Anil Kapoor) asks a new question, Jamal has a flashback. Each flashback gives Jamal clues while simultaneously providing the film's audience with another chapter of his life story. I'm not giving anything away here. Suffice it to say that the movie would be pretty short if Jamal didn't have an uncanny ability to keep playing.

So, for example, one question is: "What face appears on an American hundred dollar bill?" Prem is certain that no *chai wallah* can possibly know the answer to this question, so when Jamal says "Benjamin Franklin," Prem is astonished. Of course, as soon as Prem responds ("You're right!"), we're bombarded with flashing lights and jazzy sound effects, but this is a triumphant cinematic moment because Jamal's ability to draw strength from his piteous circumstances gives us all hope. Members of the onscreen audience rejoice simply because Jamal knows the answer, and knowing the answer allows him to keep playing for ever higher stakes. But members of the film audience are even more exhilarated because we see why he knows, and that makes us the real beneficiaries of Jamal's success.

Slumdog Millionaire rests on the shoulders of nine young actors, none of whom came to this project with significant screen experience.

- Jamal: Ayush Mahesh Khedekar plays Jamal as a kid, Tanay Hemant Chheda plays Jamal as an adolescent, and Dev Patel plays Jamal as a teenager.

- Salim: Azharuddin Mohammed Ismail plays Jamal's brother "Salim" as a kid, Ashutosh Lobo Gajiwala plays Salim as an adolescent, and Madhur Mittal plays Salim as a teenager.

- Latika: "Latika" is an orphan girl who becomes the love of Jamal's life. Rubina Ali plays Latika as a kid, Tanvi Ganesh Lonkar plays Latika as an adolescent, and Freida Pinto plays Latika as a teenager.

These nine youngsters completely individuate themselves—we always know which one is which in every scene. From the very start, Jamal is resourceful, Salim is pugnacious, and Latika is resilient. Just watching them meet the challenges of life in modern India as they grow would be thrilling in and of itself, even without the game show hook. But starting the film with teenage Jamal (Dev Patel) facing off against Prem has one great narrative advantage: even though the odds against them seem almost insurmountable, we already know these kids are going to survive. If we didn't know this from the start, would we still let ourselves go where these filmmakers take us? Be warned: some portions of their journey will totally break your heart.

Three adult actors serve as narrative anchors. Bollywood star Anil Kapoor gives Prem a sinister glamour, Irrfan Khan (best known to First World audiences as Gogol's father, "Ashoke Ganguli," in *The Namesake)* warms up the otherwise thankless role of a police inspector called in when Prem accuses Jamal of cheating, and Ankur Vikal plays "Maman," the Fagin equivalent in the horrific *Oliver Twist*-type scenes. But the nine youngsters are the heart and soul of this film, and if any one of them had stumbled, then *Slumdog Millionaire* would never have become so much greater than the sum of its parts. Kudos to the filmmakers and their total command of the arts & sciences of cinema!

SPOILER ALERT!!!
Please do NOT read until AFTER you have seen *Slumdog Millionaire*

Regular readers know that I do not subscribe to the popular belief that a source novel is always better than its film adaptation. I can name cases where the book and the film are complementary, and I can also name cases where the film is actually superior to the book. In this case, the film *Slumdog Millionaire* is definitely better than the book.

As screenwriter Simon Beaufoy explains in the official press kit: "The biggest problem in converting the book to a screenplay was that it was effectively a series of twelve short stories. It had no over-arching narrative. Some of the stories were almost discreet little tales that had no reference to the main characters at all… My job was to find the overall narrative, to trace a storyline that went all the way through Jamal's life."

Both novel and screenplay have the same basic goal: to reveal the arc of a life though a series of quiz show questions. But even though Beaufoy takes several incidents from Swarup's novel, he creates a very different central character. Swarup's hero is an orphan named "Ram Mohammed Thomas." Ram never knows anything about either of his parents, and he has no clue if they were Hindus, Moslems, Christians, or some combination. He spends his early years in the care of a Catholic priest, and his greatest asset moving forward is his ability to speak English. Ram has a friend named Salim, but Salim is an intermittent presence, and Ram's visits to the young prostitute "Nita" pale in comparison to Jamal's chaste devotion to Latika.

Beaufoy took a good book and turned it into a great screenplay. Using Alexandre Dumas's title *The Three Musketeers* as his central image and Charles Dickens' novel *Oliver Twist* as his narrative spine, Beaufoy creates a compelling triangle built on the overlapping stories of a Muslim teenager, his brother, and the girl who is sometimes sister, sometimes bride. Tricky devil: Beaufoy never actually names the third Musketeer, but I'll save you a trip to Wikipedia. The answer is Aramis.

© **Jan Lisa Huttner (11/20/08)—Special for WomenArts**

Water
Written & Directed by Deepa Mehta
Co-written by Anurag Kashyap

Principal Actors: Lisa Ray
with John Abraham & Seema Biswas

Water, *the third part of Deepa Mehta's Elements trilogy, is a triumphant tribute to Mehta's faith in humanity despite all the reasons for despair. Once again, Mehta tells a deeply personal story set in a moment of great historical change. This time the year is 1938, and Gandhi is just beginning to mobilize the crowds that will inevitably drive the British out of India a decade later. But the widows living in an ashram in Benares (the holy city on the Ganges River now called Varanasi) are expected to renounce the world and spend their lives in mourning.*

Penny's Points: ✴✴✴✴½

Water, the third part of Deepa Mehta's *Elements* trilogy, premiered at the 2005 Toronto Film Festival after years of disappointment and delay, and is finally being released in the USA this spring. The attempt to film *Water* in India touched off waves of protests by supporters of Hindutva (Hindu cultural nationalism). When the original production in the holy city of Benares was shut down in 1999, four years passed before Mehta was able to resume filming in Sri Lanka. Audiences everywhere are now indebted to Mehta for her perseverance; *Water* is a luminous film, a triumphant tribute to Mehta's faith in humanity despite all the reasons for despair.

Deepa Mehta first achieved international prominence with the release of *Fire* in 1996. Newlyweds Jatin and Sita are both from proper middle-class families. They're expected to find satisfaction in their arranged marriage, but neither of them can. Ignored by her husband, the bride slowly develops a passionate interest in her sister-in-law Radha. Jatin's brother Ashok is a religious man and Sita assumes that Radha is equally devout, but as the two women get to know each other, Sita realizes that

Radha's spirit has been stifled by Ashok's ritualistic self-abnegation.

The release of *Fire* sent shock-waves throughout India where a lesbian relationship between two characters named after Hindu goddesses was perceived as a deliberate affront by fundamentalists. But Mehta's elegant storytelling skills and the powerfully restrained performances of her two lead actresses (Shabana Azmi and Nandita Das) were widely acclaimed in the West, and *Fire* received numerous film festival awards.

Two years later, Mehta released *Earth*, based on Bapsi Sidhwa's autobiographical novel *Cracking India*. Unlike *Fire* which is set in the vague present, *Earth* is set at a specific point in historical time: the moment right before British rule ended in 1947, prompting India and Pakistan to declare themselves separate countries.

Earth's main character is "Lenny Sethna" (Maia Sethna), the daughter of a prominent Parsee family living in the cosmopolitan city of Lahore. Lenny has been born into a very comfortable life; Hindus, Moslems, and Sikhs all dine together as friends at her parents' gracious table. But soon political disagreements intrude on her world, and Lenny watches in confusion as the adult relationships around her begin to fragment. Atrocities on all sides lead to escalating violence and inevitable tragedy.

Mehta is careful to show the unfolding horror through Lenny's innocent eyes, and told from a child's perspective the story of this one specific ethnic conflict achieves heart-breaking universality.

With *Water*, Mehta once again tells a deeply personal story set in a moment of great historical change. This time the year is 1938, and Gandhi is just beginning to mobilize the crowds that will inevitably drive the British out of India a decade later. But eight-year-old "Chuyia" (Sarala) knows nothing about any of this; she is a child beset by her own miseries. Married to a man she barely knew, Chuyia is already a widow. According to custom, her father and her mother-in-law bring her to an ashram in Benares (the holy city on the Ganges River now called Varanasi), where she is expected to renounce the world and spend the rest of her life in mourning.

For the other women in the ashram, Chuyia is an immediately destabilizing force. As they look at her, they see the children they once were, and they also see the children they will never have. "Shakuntala" (Seema Biswas), who has devoted herself to religious rituals for years, begins to ache with long-buried maternal longings. The more she tries to change Chuyia, channeling her youthful energy into "appropriate" behavior, the more Shakuntala comes to question her own choices. Does she really want Chuyia to live the same life of sacrifice and self-suppression?

The three chapters of the trilogy, which Mehta both wrote and directed, share common concerns. Like Radha in *Fire*, Shakuntala is deeply disturbed by watching a vibrant youngster rapidly age under the weight of tradition. Like Lenny in *Earth*, Chuyia becomes the unwitting facilitator of a doomed romance. But the mood of each film is set by a distinct palette keyed to its title: the glowing reds and oranges of passion in *Fire*, the dusty browns and grays of civil war in *Earth*, and the bleached white of religious asceticism in *Water*. When the widows celebrate the spring festival of Holi by throwing powdered dye on Chuyia's sari, the burst of color is almost painful.

Deepa Mehta has created unforgettable women in the course of her distinguished career. Her main characters (Lenny, Radha, and Shakuntala) all start out obedient, but their reservoirs of inner strength inspire us.

© **Jan Lisa Huttner** (5/1/06) —**Special for Digital Filmmaker**

Winter's Bone
Directed By Debra Granik
Screenplay by Granik & Anne Rosellini
(Based on a novel by Daniel Woodrell)

Starring: Jennifer Lawrence
with Dale Dickey & John Hawkes

Seventeen-year-old "Ree Dolly" (Jennifer Lawrence) is searching for her father. Born into an insular criminal world totally foreign to most of us, Ree doesn't know everything, but she knows a great deal more than we do, and it's our job to catch up. Like The Godfather Saga, Winter's Bone *transcends genre rules and creates indelible characters with great mythic resonance. But in* Winter's Bone, *we're following a girl's journey to womanhood, therefore women, not men, are always in the foreground. I doubt I'll see a better film this summer; maybe I won't see a better film all year!*

Penny's Points: ✳✳✳✳½

Seventeen-year-old "Ree Dolly" (Jennifer Lawrence) is searching for her father Jessup. At first she's looking with a weary air of resignation. After all, this is a man who has left her alone, time and again, to care for a mentally ill mother and two young siblings. But something is different now; Ree can sense it even if it takes her a while to put all the pieces together.

The characters in *Winter's Bone* come from Daniel Woodrell's 2006 source novel, adapted for the screen by director Debra Granik and her writing partner Anne Rosellini. Granik and Rosellini tell the story completely from Ree's point of view, the POV of someone born into an insular criminal world totally foreign to Granik and most of her viewers. Ree doesn't know everything, but she knows a great deal more than we do, and it's our job to catch up.

Cinematographer Michael McDonough filmed every scene on location with new digital RED, softening the harsh landscapes with sun-dappled trees, clouds of smoke, and crusts of frost.

The people all have a mythic resonance, and Granik embellishes their spare dialogue with twangy music (including vocals by folklorist Marideth Sisco) on the soundtrack. The result is a film that works equally well in two dimensions: it has the dreamlike quality of a classic fairytale (like *Little Red Riding Hood,* Ree often trudges alone through dark forests), but it also feels totally true to its own specific place and time (the Ozark hills of Southwest Missouri where methamphetamines—also called "crank" and "crystal meth"—are the current drugs of choice).

Although the criminal element provides narrative drive, it's really just a hook to draw us into Ree's world. Faced with troubles like those that plague "Michael Corleone" (Al Pacino) in *The Godfather, Part One*, Ree will never find a way to reconcile family love with the dictates of her own troubled conscience. Both Vito Corleone and Jessup Dolly courted their fate; Ree knows this, just as Michael does, but that only makes things more painful for both of them.

The Godfather Saga, like all the best crime dramas, transcended genre rules and placed plot in service to character. In this case too, Ree Dolly is on an epic American journey. But in *Winter's Bone,* we're following a girl, therefore women, not men, are always in the foreground.

Ree knows full well there are some places women should never go; she goes anyway. And women see her coming, opening their doors to her before she can knock. "Ain't you got no men could do this?" asks "Merab" (Dale Dickey) wife of the stony patriarch Thump Milton. "No, ma'am, I don't."

Every woman she meets implicitly understands Ree's predicament, and shares tiny new slivers of information. Neighbor "Sonya" (Shelley Waggener) brings food and other provisions; best friend "Gail" (Lauren Sweetser) adds car keys. Thump's granddaughter "Megan" (Casey MacLaren) provides physical protection when Ree goes to see Jessup's mean-eyed buddy; Jessup's girlfriend "April" tells what she's seen firsthand. Even Merab finally uses her power as Thump's wife on Ree's behalf. With their wind at her back, Ree presses on until she has answers as well as the physical evidence required to make her hard-won knowledge stick.

Meanwhile their men, drug-fueled and reckless, posture and preen. Early on Ree thinks she can depend on her "Uncle Teardrop" (John Hawkes), but he wants none of it. When his girlfriend "Victoria" (Cinnamon Schultz) tries to intercede, Teardrop barks at her: "I said shut up once already, with my mouth." But Ree's persistence draws Teardrop back like a moth to the flame. When Victoria mouths off in front of Ree, that's merely a private embarrassment, but Ree bloodied and bruised is a public humiliation, so Teardrop swoops in like an avenging angel, bringing them both closer to death than to answers. Sitting in the audience, we can see that volatile Uncle Teardrop is as doomed as Michael Corleone's brother "Sonny" (James Caan). Ree sees this too.

Dangers in the frigid world outside are counterpointed with intimate scenes of a surprisingly warm domestic life. Brother "Sonny" (Isaiah Stone) and sister "Ashlee" (Ashlee Thompson) follow Ree's every move with their eyes and bundle against her like pups whenever she slows down. Mother "Connie" (Valerie Richards), unable to fill a parental role, has become a third dependent, so Ree cares for her tenderly, brushing her hair and keeping her close to the stove. Drawing strength from fond memories, Ree shows her young siblings photographs of Connie, and this helps them stay bonded as a cohesive unit: "I'd get lost without the weight of you two on my back." says Ree, and it's true.

As the story moves forward, Ree encounters three adult men on the right side of the law (Garret Dillahunt as a sheriff, Tate Taylor as a bail bondsman, and Russell Schalk as an army recruiter), all of whom are heavier and more stolid in their bulk than scrawny meth-heads like Uncle Teardrop and Little Arthur. In her current circumstances, Ree must do everything possible to keep men like these at the periphery of her world. But by giving them all a padded virility, Granik shows us a light at the end of the tunnel. Ree will continue to gravitate towards their world not only for her personal safety but because she already knows her brother Sonny has no future otherwise. ("Sonny," can that name be a mere coincidence?)

For decades now, Parts One & Two of *The Godfather Saga* have been considered masterpieces of world cinema. Can *Winter's Bone* stand up to this comparison? Consider this: The release of *The Godfather, Part One* in 1973 made stars of hitherto unknown actors like Al Pacino and James Caan, and it resurrected Marlon Brando's career. *Winter's Bone* is also perfectly cast, and I predict that, come December, Jennifer Lawrence ("Ree") and John Hawkes ("Uncle Teardrop") will both find places on Oscar short-lists. If I ruled the world, Dale Dickey ("Merab") would be on those lists too.

Regular readers already know that I follow a rigid rule when reviewing adaptations: I always try to see the film first. When I enter the theatre to see a film for the first time, I want my mind to be the cleanest possible slate, but once I decide to write a full review, I read background materials and then see the film a second time before completing my review. I do NOT believe the conventional wisdom that a source book is always better than a film. In fact I have written several reviews in which I argue that the film is actually better than its source book. But more important than compare & contrast, I believe that books and films are different aesthetic experiences subject to different rules, and filmmakers must always have full latitude to make cinematically-significant decisions.

All that said, I am delighted to report that in this case, author and filmmaker have done the near impossible: created works of arts that are completely parallel and totally synergistic. Reading

Winter's Bone in novel form enhances the cinematic experience, and watching *Winter's Bone* on screen enhances the literary experience.

I urge you to share this journey with Ree. I think if you do, you'll be richly rewarded. Is this a violent story? Sometimes, yes. But as Ree says to Sonny: "There's stuff you're just gonna havta get over being scared of." Me, I doubt I'll see a better film this summer; maybe I won't see a better film all year!

© **Jan Lisa Huttner (6/24/10)—Special for WomenArts**

CHAPTER THREE
Films rated 4

"The whole is **equal** to the sum of its parts."

2 Days in Paris
Written & Directed by Julie Delpy

Principal Actors: Julie Delpy
with Adam Goldberg & Marie Pillet

Thirty-something Parisian photographer—now living in Manhattan—returns home with her latest boyfriend in tow. I laughed myself silly watching 2 Days in Paris, *but then, once Delpy had me in the palm of her hand, she and Goldberg took me someplace quite unexpected, and the ending absolutely broke my heart.*

Penny's Points: ✳✳✳✳

American audiences know Julie Delpy best as the ethereal creature who played "Celine" opposite Ethan Hawke's "Jesse" in director Richard Linklater's two indie classics *Before Sunrise* (1995) and *Before Sunset* (2004). She made her feature film debut at age 14 in Jean-Luc's Godard's *Détective* (released in 1985), and she's been a successful actress ever since, but she's wanted to do more behind-the-scenes for years now.

Before Sunset (which Delpy co-wrote with Linklater and Hawke) received an Oscar nomination for Best Adapted Screenplay and that success has finally opened new doors for her. In *2 Days in Paris*, she not only stars and directs, she also wrote the screenplay, helped produce, composed some of the music, and contributed some of the still photography. Very few women have had comparable opportunities and only Barbra Streisand has made a directing debut with more moxie. (Charming as it is though, *Paris* is still a low-budget Indie whereas Streisand's *Yentl* was a major studio release.)

The character Delpy has created for herself in *Paris* is named "Marion," and many of the facts of Marion's life mirror the facts of Delpy's life. The people playing her parent in *Paris* are, in fact, her real parents (Marie Pillet and Albert Delpy), and even "Jean-Luc," the cat, is Delpy's real pet, Max. But Marion is not Delpy; she's a fictional creation who just happens to embody qualities antithetical to those depicted in earlier roles. Totally grounded and far more salty than sweet, Marion is, in many ways, the opposite of Celine. I met Delpy when she came to Chicago in late July for a Press Day at the Four Seasons Hotel, and when I asked her about this, she agreed: "Marion is not the 'ideal creature' that Celine is."

Her romantic foil is "Jack" played by Adam Goldberg (best-known as "the Jewish guy" on the *Saving Private Ryan* team). Although he's had a very successful career playing second bananas, Goldberg has never played a serious leading role before and he handles it beautifully. On his first trip to "the city of lovers," Jack must cope with the reality of a place idealized by artists for centuries. New sights and smells are unexpectedly repugnant, and the people, far from being aloof and hypercritical, are often overly-familiar. This is especially true of Marion's parents, who treat the new man in their daughter's life as just one more in a long queue.

Many critics have compared Marion and Jack to the adorably fractious characters played by Woody Allen and Diane Keaton in *Annie Hall* (1977). Much as I love that film (one of the few comedies to ever win a Best Picture Oscar), I find very little comparison other than the obvious: Jack is definitely Jewish and Marion is not. In the context of *Paris,* it's much more important to note that these two couples are on opposite sides of the sexual revolution.

Annie, like Celine, has a winsome softness, perfectly captured by her much quoted line: "Oh, well; la de da, la de da." Marion is far more self-possessed. If Jack were to tell her which books to buy, which courses to take, and other ways to continually "improve herself" for his benefit, Marion would likely bite his head off. *Paris* is a comedy, so Delpy allows herself to push the edge of the envelope, aggressively confronting racist cab drivers and duplicitous ex-lovers with equal abandon. "You can't react always as Marion does," Delpy told me, "because otherwise you'd get in trouble all the time." But playing Marion was clearly liberating for her. ("It was so much fun... kind of like a fantasy of what I wish I could do.") And she especially enjoyed Marion's physical courage. ("Physically I'm a little woman and I don't dare.")

None of this would work if Goldberg had Allen's physique, but in fact he's quite buff and tattooed. In his only other lead role, Goldberg played "Mordechai Jefferson Carver," the eponymous hero of the 2003 blaxploitation-parody *The Hebrew Hammer,* so it's fun to watch him react every time Marion gets feisty. (I learned in other interviews that Goldberg is one of Delpy's real ex's although I never asked her about this myself.)

I laughed myself silly watching *Paris,* but then, once Delpy had me in the palm of her hand, she and Goldberg took me someplace quite unexpected, and the ending absolutely broke my heart. Like all great comediennes, Delpy knows that every deep relationship is inherently tragic, poised forever on the brink of loneliness and loss. I loved this trip to Paris: I laughed; I cried; I had a thoroughly satisfying emotional experience. And then, when I got home, I kissed my cats, and oh yes, I kissed my husband too!

© **Jan Lisa Huttner (8/23/07)—Special for WomenArts**

Anne B. Real
Written & Directed by Lisa France

Key Performances: Janice Richardson
with Carlos Leon & Jackie Quinones

Cynthia is a high school student in a dangerous urban neighborhood who finds inspiration in The Diary of Anne Frank. *Outwardly she seems quiet, but the tension within her builds until she takes dramatic public control of her own words at a rap concert.*

Penny's Points: ✳✳✳✳

"Who owns Anne Frank?" Cynthia Ozick asked, in a provocative essay she published in the *New Yorker* magazine in 1997. It's easy to agree with Ozick's attack on those who strip Anne Frank of her Jewish identity and make her into a "universal" cultural commodity. Nevertheless, no one can ignore the fact that Anne's diary has been translated into almost every common language, and millions of copies are treasured, especially by young women, around the world. Creative artists of every background will therefore continue to find their own inspiration in Anne's words with surprising results, the most recent of which is a wonderful new film called *Anne B. Real.*

A teenage girl of Afro-Caribbean heritage named Cynthia Gimenez lives in a cramped Manhattan apartment on the edge of Spanish Harlem. Her mother and grandmother speak minimal English. Her older sister is an unwed mother living on welfare. Her older brother is a drug-dealing junkie. In the course of the film, Cynthia faces chaos and betrayal. One of her buddies is deliberately murdered, while another of her loved ones is accidentally shot. She runs from the police at one point, and to them at another. But through it all, Cynthia has a secret friend: Anne Frank.

In a flashback scene early in the film, Cynthia's now-dead father gives his young daughter a dog-eared copy of *The Diary of Anne*

Frank, and for the rest of the film Anne's words, read verbatim by Cynthia, provide both her solace and her inspiration. Cynthia buys herself a plaid notebook that looks very much like Anne's original, and she retreats to her corner, like Anne did, to record her private thoughts. "All children must look after their own upbringing," she reads, and from these words she understands that she can either blame her surroundings and give up, or take responsibility for her own future.

She finds out that her brother has been selling her poems to a rapper named Deuce who has been performing them and recording them and claiming them as his own. But with Anne's voice in her head, Cynthia finds her courage, and by the end of the film she has transformed herself into an artist named "Anne B. Real."

Anne B. Real won major awards at several film festivals and was nominated for two Independent Spirit Awards this year (director Lisa France was nominated for a John Cassavetes Award for Best Feature made for under $500,000, and Janice Richardson, who plays Cynthia, was nominated for Best Debut Performance), but the film never received a theatrical release. However it is now available on DVD, and it's definitely worth tracking down.

Sensitive to the raw language which pervades hip-hop culture, Ms. France insisted that all her actors respect her intention to make a PG-rated film before they signed on. In an exclusive interview, Ms. France told the *World Jewish Digest* she had two reasons for this requirement. First she wanted the film to be suitable for everyone, including Anne's legions of young readers: "Urban family entertainment is rare. We wanted to make a film that an 8-year old and a 90-year old could watch together and we would not feel embarrassed or uncomfortable."

The second motivation was her respect for Anne Frank's legacy. When Antonio Macia, who plays one of Cynthia's teachers in the film, wrote the original screenplay, he paraphrased Anne's words. Once the film was a go, however, producer Luis Moro contacted the Anne Frank Foundation in Switzerland and received permission to quote extensively from the actual text. According to Ms. France, Bernd Elias, one of Anne's last surviving relatives and the President of the Foundation, was extremely supportive.

Would Cynthia Ozick approve of a film that explicitly compares Anne's Amsterdam annex to Cynthia's Amsterdam Avenue apartment? Probably not. But the important point is that Anne gave us specific, hard-won insights into the realities of the world she knew firsthand, and so does Cynthia. Anne was never able to tell us about her experiences in Westerbork, Auschwitz or Bergen-Belsen, so parents and teachers share responsibility for explaining exactly how and why Anne died. But we don't honor her life if we only focus on her death.

Like her heroine, Ms. France finds an artistic imperative in Anne's words. "If we're ever going to have peace in this world, we have to continue to make stories that join cultures," she said. I think Anne Frank, who pasted Hollywood photos around her bed and dreamed that her words would make her immortal, would agree.

© **Jan Lisa Huttner (4/01/04)—Special for World Jewish Digest**

Brick Lane
Directed by Sarah Gavron
Screenplay by Abi Morgan & Laura Jones
(Based on a novel by Monica Ali)

Principal Actors: Tannishtha Chatterjee
with Naeema Begum & Satish Kaushik

Haunting evocation of immigrant life, tenderly delineating the slow steps by which a Bangladeshi woman makes a home for her daughters in London so different in every way from the one she herself knew as a girl. I applaud the filmmakers' intentions, but one huge casting decision undermines their efforts.

Penny's Points: ✳✳✳✳

Brick Lane is a beautiful film that could have been even better. Based on a well-regarded novel of the same name by Monica Ali, Sarah Gavron's film is about a young Bangladeshi woman named "Nazneen," who's sent to London as a teenager to marry a man she's never met.

After a brief prologue filled with idyllic childhood scenes of Nazneen and her younger sister Hasina romping through lush greenery, the story picks up again almost twenty years later. Nazneen (played as an adult by Tannishtha Chatterjee) and her husband "Chanu" (Satish Kaushik) are now a long-married couple raising two daughters: "Shahana" and "Bibi." Bibi (Lana Rahman) is still young, sweet, and compliant, but Shahana (Naeema Begum) is a teenager with raging hormones and a sharp tongue.

Brick Lane is a real place, and it's been the center of the British garment district ever since Huguenot refugees brought their looms from France in the early 18th century, followed by waves of poor Irishmen and Ashkenazi Jews. When Chanu leaves his position on the District Council, a friend helps Nazneen connect to the neighborhood's thriving underground economy, and her new job as a home-based pieceworker brings her into regular contact with "Karim" (Christopher Simpson) the young man who brings her materials and takes her finished goods back to the factory.

The film holds fast to Nazneen's point-of-view, rewarding the viewer with a deep and multifaceted depiction of the inner life of an immigrant woman. Nazneen lives quietly day-by-day, never fully aware of the fact that her loyalties are gradually shifting in tiny increments from the past (as embodied by her spouse) to the future (as embodied by her children). Although the filmmakers always respect their source material and do their best to portray the real Brick Lane neighborhood, the core of this story is universal.

Chatterjee is a soulful actress and Nazneen is a wholly satisfying stand-in for every woman who's ever left everything familiar behind in order to build a new home in a distant place. Regardless of how she arrived, whether voluntarily, under duress, or in flight, once the immigrant woman is in the new place, her home becomes her domain. The outside world, news of which generally comes to her second-hand, has less reality than preparing food, laundering clothes, and doing all the mundane things required to nurture those who depend on her.

Gavron gets strong performances from all of her actors, and she does a brilliant job of using lights and shadows to define the interior spaces. But she threw her film visually off balance by casting Satish Kaushik as Chanu. I hate myself for saying this, but I think it has to be said: Kaushik is simply too physically unattractive to hold up his end of the narrative. The truth is that Chanu is a great guy. Even though he stomps around their tiny apartment threatening physical violence, he's actually proud of the fact that he's helped to create a modern daughter who's free to speak her mind. Unlike Nazneen, Chanu is a "true believer," devoted to English literature and higher education.

Inevitably Shahana, blunt, cruel, and totally self-absorbed, forces Chanu to face his predicament: to their British neighbors, Chanu is just another "Paki;" an immigrant with dark skin and a heavy accent; an ardent colonial with an inflated view of his own prospects. But as Nazneen learns through her relationship with Karim, even if Chanu had been handsome in youth, discrimination would have worn him down, growing ever more burdensome as he aged.

Adapting the novel for the screen, the filmmakers understood that they had to make their heroine prettier than Ali created her, but they didn't seem to anticipate how much more obese and ugly Kaushik would look standing next to someone with Chatterjee's delicate beauty. This is a tragic error. Casting Kaushik as Chanu makes it easy for audiences to dismiss his well-earned grievances, and robs the film of a hero whose worldly travails are the mirror image of this heroine's domestic triumph.

SPOILER ALERT:
Comparing novel & film versions of *Brick Lane*

Monica Ali's novel *Brick Lane* runs 415 pages, a substantial percentage of which contain letters from Hasina (Nazneen's sister in Bangladesh). Since Ali always punctuates Nazneen's story with updates from Hasina, the reader understands that Nazneen is actually "the lucky one" long before Nazneen is able to appreciate this fact for herself. In deference to those who have yet to read Ali's wonderful novel, I won't say any more here about the tragic dimensions of Hasina's life.

The novel also contains chapters about Nazneen's childhood in Bangladesh as well as her early years in London (including the death of her first child and the chronicle of Chanu's career disappointments). Important characters like Dr. Azad and Razia also get their own narrative arcs.

Bottom line: Novel and film are completely complementary, and if I ruled the world, Gavron would make a sequel in which Hasina's POV was punctuated by letters from Nazneen.

© **Jan Lisa Huttner (6/27/08)—Special for WomenArts**

Frida
Directed by Julie Taymor
Screenplay by Clancy Sigal & Diane Lake
and Gregory Nava & Anna Thomas

Principal Actors: Salma Hayek
with Alfred Molina & Geoffrey Rush

Frida Kahlo was born in Mexico City in 1907. Her mother was a Mexican Catholic. Her father was a German Jewish immigrant. When the film begins, she is a precocious adolescent. By the time of her death in 1954, she has become one of the most famous artists in the world.

Penny's Points: ✳✳✳✳

Frida is a "biopic," and like most films in this genre, the narrative line is somewhat set by the real events of the real life depicted. So the "plot outline" has Frida Kahlo's exuberant young life physically constrained after a tragic accident. Her university career is over. She will never become a doctor. The specialists tell her she will never walk again.

Of course, Frida does learn to walk. And the months and years spent as an invalid turn her inward, toward her new vocation. As her confidence as a painter grows, she demands the attention of muralist Diego Rivera, Mexico's most famous living artist. He becomes her mentor, then her lover, then her husband. Together they become one of Mexico's best known couples – icons of the bohemian Left.

As their fame grows, so do their opportunities. They move to Manhattan for awhile in the early '30s. Soon Frida's work is exhibited in Paris, and she is on the cover of *Vogue* magazine. Hollywood stars buy their paintings and political émigrés seek shelter in their home. Their marital relations wax and wane with the years, in the face of triumphs, disasters, and betrayals.

Such tales can be tedious, but this one is exhilarating because director Taymor finds magically creative ways to depict Frida's inner reality. The mise-en-scene is filled with color and light, and the soundtrack (by Taymor's life partner Elliot Goldenthal) is a sensuous amalgam of authentic folk songs and Mexican-inflected melodies.

Taymor puts her emphasis right where it should be – not on the "lives" per se but on the output. "Diego" (as played by Alfred Molina) is a huge and physically imposing man, but even he is dwarfed by the enormous walls and ceilings he covers with dynamic tributes to "the People." "Frida" (Salma Hayek) is tiny and fragile, and her canvases are dense and self-referential. For Taymor, the tension between them is best captured in Frida's fevered dreams: Diego becomes King Kong -- smacking his chest with gusto and squeezing her writhing body in his massive hands.

Taymor has found ways to move the audience in and out of Frida's work at will. Sometimes a scene will begin with live action and slowly freeze into a painting. Other times, Taymor will focus on a specific canvas, then pull back as the images literally come to life. For some artists, this would be a fool-hardy approach, but for Frida Kahlo it's perfect. In the wedding scene, for example, you can see Frida looking at her own image in the mirror and deciding, literally on the spot, how she wants to look when she paints herself as a bride. Through scenes like this the audience comes to appreciate that the "Frida" we know today is the woman she created for us in her mind's eye. Compared to that fundamental truth, who really cares which body was in which bed when?

If I have one complaint about this film, it's that the actors are somewhat overwhelmed by the spectacle. I wanted more "chemistry" between Hayek and Molina, but the sexiest scene in the film is actually a tango featuring Hayek and Ashley Judd (as Italian photographer Tina Modotti). I found most of the cameos distracting: Antonio Banderas as David Siqueros, Ed Norton as Nelson Rockefeller, Geoffrey Rush as Leon Trotsky. Why? Maybe famous names were needed to secure the necessary funding? If so, what a shame! Judd's physical charisma aside, the best acting is done by Valeria Golino as Diego's second wife (Lupe Marin). I also liked Mia Maestro as Frida's sister Cristina and Roger Rees as their father Guillermo. The family scenes have a warmth and intimacy missing in some of the "bigger" moments.

Frida is one of the best films of the year, and one of the best films ever made about an artist. Focus on Frida and Diego as artists rather than "personalities," and you will be thoroughly mesmerized.

© **Jan Lisa Huttner (11/30/02)—Special for DVDWolf**

Heir to an Execution
Documentary by Ivy Meeropol

Key Participants: Ivy Meeropol
with Michael & Robert Meeropol

Documentary about Ethel & Julius Rosenberg, executed in 1953 for "stealing the secret of the atom bomb." Fifty years after the Rosenberg's execution, their granddaughter, Ivy Meeropol, reflects on their lives, principles, and ultimate sacrifice.

Penny's Points: ✳✳✳✳

On June 19, 1953, a 36-year-old Jewish woman with two small children was electrocuted at Sing Sing Prison in Ossining, New York. Fifty-one years later, her granddaughter's new documentary film *Heir to an Execution* is about to broadcast nationwide on cable television behemoth HBO.

The grandmother was the infamous Ethel Rosenberg; the granddaughter is Ivy Meeropol, daughter of Ethel's oldest son, Michael. (After their parents were executed, Michael and his younger brother Robert were adopted by New York songwriter Abel Meeropol and his wife Anne.)

When the film airs for the first time on June 14, 2004, critics and pundits will no doubt use the occasion to debate, yet again, questions of guilt or innocence. Like her father and uncle before her, Ms. Meeropol will probably be labeled an apologist for her refusal to focus on what we now know (or think we know) about Julius Rosenberg's espionage career. But Ms. Meeropol herself is far more interested in questions of context and consequences. She is now a woman in her mid-thirties, and she will soon be older than her grandmother ever lived to be. Watching the film, it is clear that this fact haunts her.

In an effort to understand her grandparents as people rather than symbols, Ms. Meeropol seeks out the comrades of their youth. Luckily for us, many of them are still with us, (including the remarkable Harry Steingart, 103 years old when Ms. Meeropol interviews him). Like Steingart, most of the Rosenbergs' friends were trade unionists and/or members of the American Communist Party. And every single one of them, Miriam Moskowitz, Abe Osheroff, Morty Sobell, etc., etc., was Jewish.

These elderly activists, looking back now at events which occurred two full generations ago, may or may not be remembering all the details with pinpoint accuracy. After all, many of the stories they tell have probably been told dozens of times before and therefore have an almost mythical quality. But the world they evoke is beyond dispute. To paraphrase Osheroff when he describes the Rosenbergs' wedding: "You can smell the pickled herring!"

In conjunction with the film clips and still photos Ms. Meeropol has found to illustrate these narratives, her interviews remind us of a time when thousands of young Jewish-Americans proudly dedicated their lives to the cause of universal social justice. Coming of age during the Great Depression of the 1930s, they were determined to end the poverty and oppression which surrounded them. They organized, marched, and fought for better working conditions and social services. Their enemy was never the United States government per se, it was always the plutocracy.

Were they idealistic to a fault with respect to the Soviet Union? Without doubt. Did they play a role in making our country a better place in which to live? Yes again. Without this context, it is impossible to understand why the Rosenbergs did what they did, as well as how they had the fortitude to endure once they were singled out, tried, and sentenced to death.

(Personally, I doubt we will ever be 100% certain of the facts of the case, but it appears likely that Julius Rosenberg provided our wartime allies in the Soviet Union with non-atomic military intelligence during World War II, and that Ethel knew about this even though she was not personally involved in his activities. What they were actually charged with, in 1950, was "conspiracy to commit espionage," with the apparent goal of forcing them to name other names higher up. In the court of public opinion, however, they were damned for "stealing the secret of the atom bomb," thereby endangering the survival of the United States during the Cold War.)

The Rosenbergs' friends are one half of Ms. Meeropol's story; their families constitute the other half. But while the friends are out-going, loquacious, and thoroughly individuated, family members are almost invisible, even in film clips. History books tell us that Ethel Greenglass had three brothers and Julius Rosenberg was one of five children, but neither family wants anything to do with the Meeropols. Ms. Meeropol does her best to track her cousins down and solicit their participation, to no avail. She shows herself on the phone working off of two hand-drawn family trees, but she never shows us any of the names or tells us exactly who she is talking to at any one time. Their absence therefore becomes their identity.

Finally one man in early middle-age agrees to see her. She identifies him verbally as "Barry Roberts," son of Julius's brother David. Ms. Meeropol flies to an unnamed city to meet with him in his comfortable suburban home. He is astonished when she tells him that none of the other cousins will speak with her, even off camera. He cries and she comforts him. Although the trigger events happened long before any of them were born, Ivy and Barry share a moment of sorrow for all the relatives who still live with their conflicted feelings.

Is "Rosenberg" a name to be proud of or a name that carries shame? This is the question Ms. Meeropol asks in attempting to assess the consequences of the way her grandparents chose to live and die. The Rosenberg friends seek the light. They have no fear of the past, talk honestly about the time they served in prison, and still believe in the justice of their old causes. The Rosenberg and Greenglass families hide in the shadows. Ethel's younger brother David Greenglass, the man whose testimony did the most to convict her, is shown in disguise in recent clips from the CBS newsmagazine *60 Minutes II*. Over eighty now, he lives under a false name, in total anonymity. "Because of the position Ethel and Julius took, we [the Meeropols] all get to live a life where we're proud," concludes Ms. Meeropol in her final on camera conversation with her father Michael.

In the post-9/11 world, we live once again in a time of fear and danger. What we do now has consequences. Someday each one of us will look back at this time, and we will think about what we did or didn't do, what we said or didn't say, how we voted or didn't vote. It is impossible to watch this film without asking oneself: will I be proud or will I be ashamed? Without ever defining a target, this is a question Ivy Meeropol aims straight at the heart of the Jewish-American community.

© Jan Lisa Huttner (11/01/04)—Special for World Jewish Digest

Jennifer's Body
Directed by Karyn Kusama
Screenplay by Diablo Cody

Principal Actors: Amanda Seyfried
with Megan Fox & Johnny Simmons

Rock band decides to sacrifice a virgin in hopes of getting the devil invested in their career prospects. But they pick the wrong girl, and gruesome, gory, utterly hilarious consequences ensue. You can almost hear director Karyn Kusama (Girlfight) *and screenwriter Diablo Cody* (Juno) *laughing on the soundtrack—baiting their audience with kissing babes and gallons of fake blood. Cody and Kusama gleefully subvert a century's worth of horror film tropes… and me? I'm laughing too!*

Penny's Points: ✵✵✵✵

"Nikolai Wolf," the kohl-eyed lead singer of *Low Shoulder*, is oh so tired of playing in backwater bars. When he learns that their next gig will take them to Devil's Kettle, MN, Nikolai (Adam Brody) has a brainstorm: find a virgin, sacrifice her at the eponymous waterfall, and surely Satan himself will soon come a callin'.

Wholesome blonde "Needy" (Amanda Seyfried) screams in terror as her BFF "Jennifer" is lured away, and even though she's used to having her way with men, sultry brunette "Jennifer" (Megan Fox) is a bit afraid too. But she gets into *Low Shoulder*'s black-window van anyway.

Sorry, Nikolai: you picked the wrong girl! The joke is on you and gruesome, gory, utterly hilarious consequences ensue.

I did my best to walk into the theatre open-minded. On the one hand, I'm a big fan of director Karyn Kusama. I loved her first film *Girlfight*, and I also enjoyed her second film *Aeon Flux* a great deal. (Despite negative spin from film critics, *Aeon Flux* actually did pretty well at the box office, especially compared to other women-directed films released in the past decade.)

On the other hand, I hated *Juno*, so the very thought of seeing a new film by screenwriter Diablo Cody set my teeth on edge. But even as I watched *Juno* for the first time (and then the second time), I always had the nagging suspicion that lots of, ahem, "rough edges" had been smoothed out along the way. Despite Oscar nominations all around, in my own heart I never quite believed that Juno's creator had intended her to be quite as cute and cuddly as Ellen Paige played her.

So watching the onscreen relationship between Jennifer Check and Anita "Needy" Lesnicky was pure pleasure for me. Megan Fox is best-known as "the girl" in the *Transformers* series (a part that required a beautiful body), and Amanda Seyfried is best-known as "the daughter" in *Mama Mia* (a part that required a sweet face). Between the crashing cars in the first and the ebullient elders in the second, both young actresses needed little more in their acting repertoire than firm command of reaction shots. But both Jennifer and Needy are multi-dimensional characters who grow and change as this new film unfolds.

In her opening voice-over, Needy tells us she and Jennifer have been together since their sandbox days, and they both wear matching heart-shaped BFF necklaces to prove it. (BFF means "Best Friends Forever" in cyber-speak.) But with all the pressures imposed by disparate high school cliques, childhood loyalty is an ever distant memory.

Needy is conflicted: she's certainly aware of the fact that Jennifer uses her for cover (Jennifer thinks she looks especially luscious when she's standing next to nerdy Needy), but Needy still likes going on adventures otherwise above her station.

When Jennifer asks Needy to accompany her to *The Carousel* on the fateful night, Needy's boyfriend "Chip" (Johnny Simmons) is baffled. Needy won't stay home with him because she has to go out with Jennifer? And she has to dress down in order to make Jennifer shine? It makes no sense to him. Well, of course not. Chip is not, hasn't been, and will never be a teenage girl! But Needy's always understood the quid pro quo in her relationship with Jennifer, and she's always been willing to pay to play until the trip to *The Carousel* changes everything.

Unleashing mayhem, Cody and Kusama gleefully subvert a century's worth of horror film tropes: this time girls are the monsters and boys are the victims. Jennifer easily seduces her prey (first the jock, then the goth), and with each conquest, her long, beautiful hair becomes ever more lustrous. Needy notices immediately (a touch of envy beneath her alarm). Maybe there's a tear in the universe, but there are no split ends in Jennifer's coiffure.

But her new powers grow boring, so a lonely Jennifer flirts with Needy, pouncing on her like a cat attacking a toy mouse. Enraged when Needy still keeps her distance, Jennifer zeroes in on Chip, until finally Needy understands that it's up to her to save the day.

You can almost hear Cody and Kusama laughing on the soundtrack - baiting their audience with kissing babes and gallons of fake blood. And me? I'm laughing too, even when I'm biting down on my sweater, squeamish every time Jennifer bares her fangs.

I especially love the moment when Needy breaks out of the loony bin to pursue *Low Shoulder*. It's a riff on the famous ending scene in *One Flew Over the Cuckoo's Nest*, where "Chief Bromden" (played by Will Samson) makes his great escape. *Cuckoo's Nest* received five Oscars, including Best Picture of 1976, but it's one of the most misogynistic films I've ever seen, so the brief homage in this context literally tickled me pink.

Comedy often defines the line between who's in and who's out. If you really get the joke, you can't help laughing. If you sit there stone-faced ("I get that it's a joke, but it isn't funny."), then maybe you get it in your head, but you don't get it in your gut, in other words, you really don't get it. I say this after listening to jokes for years and years and years that left me cold (or worse)—yes, I knew they were supposed to be "funny," but to me they sounded anti-Semitic or misogynistic or racist or crude or just plain dumb. Whatever . . . I laughed my head off at *Jennifer's Body* and I hope you do too.

© **Jan Lisa Huttner (9/22/09)—Special for WomenArts**

La Petite Jerusalem
Written & Directed by Karin Albou

Principal Actors: Fanny Valette
with Sonia Tahar and Elsa Zylverstein

Two sisters share a close relationship with each other, and both have warm feelings for their mother, but the enforced intimacy of their tight living situation is the source of escalating friction. This is writer/director Karin Albou's first film, and she's been showered with critical praise. Albou's achievement is immense.

Penny's Points: ✳✳✳✳

Recent revelations about Virginia Senator George Allen's Tunisian heritage have drawn American attention to the Sephardim of North Africa, but the French got there first, awarding a Cannes Film Festival prize to the delicate film *La Petite Jerusalem* in May 2005. Released in selected American art houses in early 2006, *La Petite Jerusalem* is now available to all on DVD.

While most educated Americans know that approximately 700,000 Palestinians fled from the newly-declared state of Israel in 1948, few know that Jews in most Islamic countries also lost their homes. (I have no wish here to defend either set of circumstances both of which are tremendously complex and controversial. My basic position is simply this: when a huge population of men, women, and children leave their homes and migrate, some do so by choice, but most do so under duress because they believe they have no choice.) Jews from the Anglophone countries (Egypt, India/Pakistan, Iran, Iraq, etc.) typically went either to Israel or to another English-speaking country (Australia, Canada, South Africa, USA, etc), while most of the Jews from the Francophone countries (Algeria, Lebanon, Morocco, Tunisia, etc.) went either to Israel or to France. So many Sephardic Jews now live in the Parisian suburb of Sarcelle that one of its neighborhoods is known as "little Jerusalem."

The family depicted in *La Petite Jerusalem* lives comfortably but on the edge. "Mathilde" (Elsa Zylverstein), her husband "Ariel" (Bruno Todeschini), and their four children share an apartment with Mathilde's mother and her sister "Laura" (Fanny Valette).

Like most Tunisian Jews, Mathilde is highly observant. She keeps kosher, covers her head whenever she leaves the house, regularly attends the mikva (ritual bath), and makes a concerted effort to raise her children in the embrace of Orthodox traditions. Laura, however, is a college student, responsible only for herself; she thinks of herself as more "French" than "Jewish," and thereby allows herself to mentally entertain scandalous intellectual and emotional options.

The two sisters share a close relationship with each other, and both have warm feelings for their mother (she's never give a name in the film, and always referred to as "La Mere"), but the enforced intimacy of their tight living situation is the source of escalating friction. Laura wants to move into her own apartment, but she has no money and Ariel claims he has little to spare.

The film is entirely present tense. Although Mathilde asks "La Mere" (Sonia Tahar) for details about her life in Tunisia, La Mere is like Mrs. Allen: she's put it behind her and has no wish to look back. We never learn the circumstances of her emigration, how long she's been in France, or even where her children were born. (Laura was probably born in France and is therefore a French citizen, but Mathilde, already the mother of four, is significantly older and may well have emigrated with her mother.) Nevertheless, La Mere still harbors old world superstitions, and invokes spells and talismans to "cure" Laura of her dangerous preoccupations.

This is writer/director Karin Albou's first film, and she's been showered with critical praise. In addition to winning the Cannes Film Festival "SACD Screenwriting Award" and the French Syndicate of Cinema Critics "Best First Film" award, she was also nominated for a Cesar for "Best First Work" as well as a "Golden Iris" from the Brussels European Film Festival. (Fanny Valette also received a Cesar nomination for "Most Promising Young Actress" for her portrayal of Laura.)

Albou's achievement is immense. La Mere is woman with no name and no place of her own (a sure sign of metaphorical intentions on the part of her creator). In the course of examining how each daughter incorporates her mother's complex trajectory into her own life, Albou depicts a community under siege--from within and without--with delicacy and nuance, empathy and deep respect.

© **Jan Lisa Huttner (9/30/06)—Special for Digital Filmmaker**

Little Miss Sunshine
Directed by Jonathan Dayton & Valerie Faris
Screenplay by Michael Arndt

Principal Actors: Abigail Breslin
with Toni Collette & Greg Kinnear

When six Hoovers stuff themselves into an old VW bus and head west, they're a thoroughly modern family, that is a non-nuclear mishmash. But when Olive suddenly advances to the final round of the Little Miss Sunshine Pageant, it's all or nothing; everyone must go or no one can go, so off they go. "Hilarious consequences ensue," and by the grand finale they've all taken the Three Musketeers pledge: "One for all, and all for one."

Penny's Points: ✳✳✳✳

Heads up, readers: be prepared for a million references to Leo Tolstoy's famous line "Happy families are all alike; every unhappy family is unhappy in its own way." (the opening line of *Anna Karenina*) as the Sundance crowd-pleaser *Little Miss Sunshine* begins its run at a theater near you.

The assertion itself, so simply put, is open to question. In the hundred years since Tolstoy's death in 1910, countless anthropologists, economists, political scientists, psychologists, and sociologists have all done academic research, and polemicists have addressed the topic from every possible perspective from religious fundamentalism to radical feminism. At this point, who among us would dare to declare that any individual family, including our own, was either "happy" or "unhappy" full stop?

Creative artists were mining family life for great material even before Sophocles wrote *Oedipus Rex,* and will no doubt continue to do so. As post-Freudians, however, we should just accept the simple fact that the average family will have its tragic days and its comic days and probably also experience every gradation in between.

When the six Hoovers stuff themselves into an old VW bus and head west, they're a thoroughly modern family, that is a non-nuclear mishmash. In this and so many other ways they're much closer to "the Joads" (who took a similar path to the new "promised land" of California in *The Grapes of Wrath),* than to that '50s exemplar "the Cleavers" of *Leave it to Beaver* fame. "Sheryl" and "Richard" (Toni Collette and Greg Kinnear) have a daughter (Abigail Breslin), but Sheryl also has a son from her first marriage (Paul Dano) and a gay brother (Steve Carell), while Richard brings his father (Alan Arkin) into the mix.

At the beginning of the film, all of these characters exist in their own individual bubbles. Only Sheryl, the typically over-stressed middle-class Mom, puts any priority on the ties that bind them all together. But when Olive suddenly advances to the final round of the "Little Miss Sunshine" pageant, it's all or nothing; everyone must go or no one can go, so off they go. "Hilarious consequences ensue," and by the grand finale they've all taken the Three Musketeers pledge: "One for all, and all for one." Haven't we seen all this before? Actually, no.

What distinguishes *Little Miss Sunshine* is the directors' commitment to real life. Even though every scene is grounded in those that came before it and the final scene is a foregone conclusion, the trajectory still supports several pleasant surprises and the film has many tiny moments that are refreshingly unpredictable – just like real life.

Little Miss Sunshine was directed by the husband-and-wife team of Jonathan Dayton and Valerie Faris. This is their feature debut after years of success directing music videos and television shows such as the Emmy-nominated comedy series *Mr. Show with Bob and Dave.* Married for over 17 years, Dayton and Faris bring to the screen evidence of a successful partnership built on constant communication and openness to multiple points of view. The result is a film that's genuinely "lived in," and I loved it.

I confess that I'm often annoyed by films about kids. I hate watching films in which kids do things kids don't ever really do and seem to know things they couldn't possibly know. So when I tell you that Olive completely won me over, I'm telling you a fact that surprised me. She's no mere "ugly duckling" in the beauty pageant context, she's the fish who's totally out of water, and yet her inner spark is irresistible and her love of life is totally contagious. Will the other contestants in the "Little Miss Sunshine" pageant (played not by actresses but by girls from actual beauty pageants) hate this film when they see it? I suspect that those who love pageants for their own sake, as Olive clearly does, will also love the film, but those who compete primarily to satisfy others will hate it. Olive loves to perform, and the rest of the Hoovers pull themselves together for her sake; sometimes you win just by showing up.

So ignore the critics who reduce *Little Miss Sunshine* to a comedy about a dysfunctional family. The Hoover family simply functions "in its own way," just like yours and mine.

© **Jan Lisa Huttner (7/31/06) —Special for Digital Filmmaker**

My Grandfather's House
Documentary by Ron Steinman & Eileen Douglas

Key Participants: Eileen Douglas
with her Mom & Daughter

Travel with a Jewish-American woman back to "the Old Country." Seventy-minute film has three parts. First, Eileen develops detailed information about her grandfather's family. Then she walks the streets of Lithuania he once called home. Finally, she brings all the surviving cousins together for a reunion. Wise, life-affirming, heart-warming doc.

Penny's Points: ✳✳✳✳

My Grandfather's House: A Journey Home is the story of a woman in early middle age who develops a deep craving for roots. Eileen, who narrates the story under the direction of Ron Steinman, jumps right in with minimal background. We don't know who she is or what triggered all of this, but her story has such narrative drive that we're quickly engaged.

Eileen was raised in Syracuse, New York. Her grandfather, who died when she was twelve, was a man with secrets. Whenever Eileen asked him about his family, all he would say was they "died in the War." A good little American girl, Eileen imagined it all as a movie; a bomb comes down on a house and poof, Sam's family is gone. But as an adult she finds albums filled with old pictures and letters written in Yiddish, and she becomes obsessed.

The 70-minute film is divided into three parts. In the first half-hour, Eileen plans her trip to Lithuania, assembling her grandfather's family tree. Working with a Lithuanian archivist, Eileen spends the second half hour walking the streets of Kovno and learning the details of the family's life. "This family was subject to all of the insanity of the 20th century," says one cousin in voiceover. "I can see now why my grandfather never talked," concludes Eileen.

And yet there she is, in a place that was once behind the Iron Curtain, a place all her relatives thought was lost forever. And so she decides her true mission is "To repair, to fix, to right the pain. To put loved ones torn from each other back together again, if not in this world then in another dimension."

Eileen brings all the surviving cousins together for a reunion outside Tel Aviv. It turns out that "the lucky ones" include those deported to Siberia by Stalin as well as those born in America. "Alts is rekht," they agree, and in this wise and heartwarming movie, it's true: in the end, "Everything is OK."

© Jan Lisa Huttner (1/01/05)—Special for World Jewish Digest

Red Riding Hood
Directed by Catherine Hardwicke
Screenplay by David Johnson
(Based on a folk tale from the Brothers Grimm)

Principal Actors: Amanda Seyfried
with Julie Christie & Gary Oldman

A heroine created in the Victorian Era has indelibly imprinted herself on our cultural imagination. Her basic problem is the same problem every young person must face: who can she trust? Here in the early 21st Century, "Valerie" (aka "Red Riding Hood") has a feisty core of self-reliance, so she learns to trust her own instincts, staying faithful to those who truly care for her, and keeping her distance from those who would use her for their own purposes. Can any girl do more? Director Catherine Hardwicke has deliberately created Red Riding Hood for the multiplex crowd, with a visual design that evokes a lavishly illustrated story book. She sets her story in purely imaginary landscape intended to transport us to a time long ago and a place far away. So please don't buy a ticket if you're looking for "realism." I left the theatre aesthetically and emotionally satisfied, convinced once again that no one knows my inner teenager quite as well as Catherine Hardwicke.

Penny's Points: ✳✳✳✳

Director Catherine Hardwicke has deliberately structured *Red Riding Hood* as a fairy tale visually designed to evoke a lavishly illustrated story book. The camera swoops like an eagle over a medieval landscape, circling around a town built on a rushing river, and then traveling over miles and miles of dense forest, before settling down inside a small village. But there are no longitude/latitude coordinates to identify this locale on Google Earth; this is a purely imaginary landscape intended to transport us to a time long ago and a place far away.

Summer flowers fill the screen with big splashes of color, then winter comes and the ground is quickly covered with white crystals. Do these actors live inside a snow globe? Everything here is picaresque so be warned: If you're looking for realism, you've come to the wrong movie. European peasants never wore clothes so bright and flouncy; women's hair could not have been this bounteous before shampoos, conditioners, and curling irons.

But then fear runs riot once "the wolf" begins attacking humans again (after an unexplained hiatus measured in decades). And when the villagers respond by searching for "the evil" in their midst, summoning self-righteous saviors in clerical garb and accusing each other of sorcery, we know historians all affirm exactly these responses to pervasive terror. It is precisely because *Red Riding Hood* embodies fundamental truths that we keep returning to it over and over again; here Valerie's story is a metaphor, part dream and part nightmare.

I didn't guess the wolf's identity until it revealed itself at the very end of the film. One reason I went back a second time before writing this review was to see if I'd missed any obvious clues. Then I asked others and they didn't know either. So I applaud screenwriter David Johnson for hiding his wolf in plain sight, and keeping his mystery potent well into Act Three. I also enjoyed the way he incorporated inevitable lines into the dialogue. Going in, for example, I was sure that I would hear the words "Grandmother, what big eyes you have!" at some point, but when they finally came, I was giddy with delight.

Valerie's problem is a problem every young person must face: whom can she trust? Someone in this village is the wolf. Is it one of her suitors? It is one of her friends? Is the wolf a member of her own family? Valerie has good reason to suspect everyone. She knows she is in danger, but she is no longer sure who is an enemy and who is a friend. Valerie learns to trust her instincts, stay faithful to those who truly care for her, and keep her distance from those who would use her for their own purposes. Can any girl do more?

Amanda Seyfried anchors the film, turning in another luminous performance as Valerie. This young star (still in her twenties) has made some very bold choices since her 2008 breakthrough in *Mama Mia!* She frequently works with female filmmakers (either in the screenwriter and/or director role), and she's building quite a resume even though some of her films have been commercial disasters.

Julie Christie (as "Grandmother") and Gary Oldman (as "Father Solomon") provide gravitas with tongue-in-cheek brio; Virginia Madsen and Billy Burke are appropriately mismatched as Valerie's parents; Shiloh Fernandez (as "Peter") and Max Irons (as "Henry") are virile and stalwart suitors, and Seyfried has good chemistry with both of them.

Finally there's Lukas Haas. Way back in 1985 (the year Seyfried was born!), a little boy stole our hearts as the Amish kid in *Witness*, but he hasn't been this well-used on the big screen since. As "Father Auguste," the village priest who thinks Father Solomon has answers but soon learns otherwise, Haas's enormous eyes are truly the windows of a tortured soul.

Bottom line: I left the theatre aesthetically and emotionally satisfied, convinced once again that no one knows my inner teenager quite as well as Catherine Hardwicke.

SPOILER ALERT!!!
Please do NOT read until after you've seen *Red Riding Hood*

Little Red Riding Hood is a Brothers Grimm fairy tale barely three pages long. Therefore many plot elements must be added to craft a coherent screenplay.

Two points about this adaptation of *Red Riding Hood*:

A quick trip to Wikipedia will show that many plot elements added to this version are grounded in prior iterations, for example, the idea that this "wolf" is a supernatural creature (a werewolf) rather than a wilderness creature (Genus Canis/Species Lupus).

Plot elements that are not in prior iterations, for example, the sudden appearance of Henry-the-Blacksmith as a rival for Valerie's affections, come straight from the conventions of Victorian fiction. (See my review of *Jane Eyre*.)

What I like best is how well this version explains the trips to Grandmother. I now understand not only why Grandmother lives so far away from the village, but how she managed to stay alive so long. New generations will be raised to believe that Grandmother was a witch and now Valerie herself is also a witch; people in the village will never appreciate that their own safety depends on Valerie's ability to keep the wolf domesticated.

© **Jan Lisa Huttner (3/15/11)—Special for WomenArts**

The Runaways
Written & Directed by Floria Sigismondi
(Based on a memoir by Cherie Currie)

Principal Actors: Dakota Fanning & Kristen Stewart
with Riley Keough & Michael Shannon

In Floria Sigismondi's new film The Runaways, *Dakota Fanning and Kristen Stewart play archetypes: two wide-eyed innocents, fractured halves of one whole, negotiating the drug-fueled, gender-bending, mind-blowing '70s. How much is historically true? Who cares? The* Runaways *is a feature film, not a documentary, and what moved me most were the performances. That said, writer/director Floria Sigismondi and her team have all worked very hard to capture* The Runaways' *actual milieu. Countless films have depicted the role rock music played in breaking down racial barriers, now Sigismondi has done the same for feminism. And through their brilliant portrayals of Cherie Currie and Joan*

Jett, Dakota Fanning and Kristen Stewart will now inspire a whole new generation of girls. Bravi!

Penny's Points: ✳✳✳✳

Floria Sigismondi's new film *The Runaways* is a fairy tale about two teenagers on the cusp of womanhood. Yes, it's based on Cherie Currie's memoir *Neon Angel*, and yes, it depicts real events in the lives of Currie and her *Runaways* band mate Joan Jett, but the strength of this film lies in its evocation of archetypes, not its recreation of history.

Just like in the Brothers Grimm classic *Snow-White and Rose-Red*, "Cherie" (Dakota Fanning) is a somewhat passive blonde, whereas "Joan" (Kristen Stewart) is a more adventurous brunette. They find each other in a Los Angeles punk club in 1975 when they're both 15-years-old. Cherie has tarted up with provocative clothing and heavy make-up; Joan has turned androgynous in a stylized biker outfit. They're complements, two eager innocents who are fractured halves of one whole. Eyes lock in the crowd; there's an immediate connection, but they're both too reticent to act on it.

The catalyst who bonds them together is rock impresario "Kim Foley" (Michael Shannon). Joan has been teaching herself to play electric guitar and when she meets Foley, he sees dollar signs. First he connects her with drummer "Sandy West" (Stella Maeve), and when he's sure they can really play, he sets out in search of a lead singer. He spots Cherie though the smoke-filled haze and Joan's whole face lights up. Bingo! Add two more guitars (Scout Taylor-Compton playing "Lita Ford" and Alia Shawkat playing a fictional composite character named "Robin"), and rock's first successful all-girl group snaps into place.

But first hours of practice in a decrepit trailer, while Foley screams, threatens and cajoles. Sometimes he mocks and humiliates them, other times he seduces them with soft words and pseudo-concern. Step-by-step, they advance from house parties to road trips, then a record deal, and finally a climactic tour in Japan. And all the while, the bond between Cherie and Joan grows ever stronger.

How much of this is historically true? Who cares? *The Runaways* is a feature film, not a documentary.

What moved me most were the performances. We've all watched these two girls grow up on screen. Dakota Fanning has been a star since the age of 7 when she played Sean Penn's daughter "Lucy" in *I Am Sam* in 2001. Kristen Stewart has also spent years in high profile projects (starting with the role of Jodi Foster's daughter "Sarah" in *Panic Room* in 2002), recently breaking through as "Bella" in the phenomenally successful *Twilight* saga. Like the characters they play in *The Runaways,* Fanning and Stewart are both at a perilous age now. Can they leave childhood behind and become women on screen? Leaving the theatre after *The Runaways,* my answer is a resounding yes!

Playing Cherie, Fanning gives an aggressive, gutsy, "in your face" performance. Her edge is so sharp that sometimes she almost draws blood. But raw scenes of her strutting on stage as "Cherie Bomb" are counterbalanced by tender scenes at home with her twin sister "Marie" (Riley Keough). There's a moment near the end when Joan calls her "a bruised peach," and it's a perfect description.

Stewart's performance as Joan is more interior but ultimately just as charismatic. She must convince us that she's watching and thinking and learning every minute of every day, and she does. After all, if we know anything historical coming into this film, we know it will be Joan Jett, not Cherie Currie, who eventually makes it into the top echelon of the Rock 'n Roll pantheon with her next band *Joan Jett and the Blackhearts.*

Of course, even though I sincerely believe that historicity in itself is ultimately irrelevant in a feature film, that doesn't mean that director Floria Sigismondi and her team haven't all worked very hard to capture *The Runaways'* actual milieu. In fact, they've scrupulously recreated the look and feel of the mid-70s from a feminist perspective. And Cherie Currie and Joan Jett both made themselves fully available to the team, most especially to the two young actresses portraying them.

Me, I never got anywhere close to the belly of the Rock 'n Roll beast, but I am the right age to remember how it all appeared from the sidelines. This was a time of political turmoil all around the world, and people experimented with new social and sexual identities by literally painting them on. Girls who really wanted to "be somebody" had no choice but to reach out for male role models: in *The Runaways,* Cherie mimics David Bowie while Joan transforms herself into a mini Marlon Brando.

In addition to directing, Sigismondi also wrote the screenplay, and she peppers it with dozens of tiny revealing incidents. Joan pays a teacher for electric guitar lessons, but after taking her money, he still insists girls can only play soft acoustic. When Cherie appears on stage for the first time, her classmates abuse her. Kim Foley hires local kids to impersonate hecklers; disgusting as these boys are, *The Runaways'* real crowds are far worse than the simulation. These moments combine to add cumulative force.

I remember; I was there. Growing up in the '60s, I had books about Joan of Arc on the one hand and images of countless wives and mothers on the other. I knew nurse and teacher were the only professions most women could aspire to—even most Catholic nuns were either nurses or teachers.

But Joan Jett really was one of the women who changed all of that forever. I loved watching her on MTV in the '80s (one of the only women I ever saw on MTV in the '80s), and I can easily picture myself, thrilled and exhilarated, dancing around my room in wild abandon. Joan Jett's voice gave me courage then; she still gives me courage today. And though their brilliant portrayals of Cherie Currie and Joan Jett, Dakota Fanning and Kristen Stewart will now inspire a whole new generation of girls.

Countless films have depicted the role rock music played in breaking down racial barriers, now Sigismondi has done the same for feminism. Brava!

SPOILER ALERT!!!
Please do NOT read until AFTER you have seen *The Runaways*

Sex & Drugs & Rock 'n Roll: yes, indeed, there's a great deal of all three in *The Runaways!* Everyone involved in front of the camera as well as behind it has worked extremely hard to capture *The Runaways'* actual milieu, and that **is** the way it was. So why am I recommending it so highly, and fervently hoping that a new generation of girls will be as inspired by *The Runaways* (as embodied here by Dakota Fanning and Kristen Stewart) as I was watching *Joan Jett and the Blackhearts* on MTV?

Of course, I'm not a parent, so I don't have to make decisions for children of my own. But as I've already said in several recent reviews (e.g., *An Education, Fish Tank* & *The Lovely Bones)*, I sincerely believe girls are more endangered by the things they don't know than the things they do.

The "Kim Foley" character in *The Runaways* is an expert manipulator. I have no idea how closely he resembles "the real" Kim and I frankly don't care. The character on screen (the only "Kim" I can judge) certainly bullies and harasses "his girls" emotionally, and there's no doubt he's financially exploiting them as well.

So why do they put up with it? First, of course, they're kids. Kim has all the power (reputation, connections, etc, etc); they have none.

In Sigismondi's version of this story, "Cherie" is also motivated by thwarted love for an alcoholic father. She craves attention, and that's precisely what makes her such a great performer on stage. Kim recognizes her vulnerability and preys on it. In one revealing scene, he tricks her into a solo photo shoot. I shuddered when I heard him disarm her by softening his voice. This creep knows just what he's doing!

Sigismondi's "Joan," on the other hand, lives and breathes only for her music, so she consciously apprentices herself to someone successful enough to open doors. Stewart portrays Joan as preternaturally intelligent, disciplined, and determined. She knows that Kim is her way in; furthermore, she's able to accept the fact that his noxious methods are actually great preparation (even when he pelts her with dry dog turds during his "heckler drill"). Faced with real hecklers later, Joan revels in her ability to bat incoming right back to sender.

Again, I'm putting these names in quotes to stress the fact that I'm referring to film characters, not real people. I don't know any of these people, so I cannot and will not judge them.

Nonetheless, facts are facts: Joan Jett is now one of the best-known, most accomplished women in Rock history, while Cherie Currie has gone through hard times and made it safely to the other side. What Sigismondi shows in *The Runaways* is that girls can learn to say NO, and thereby mature into successfully self-directed adult women. So me, I thank Floria Sigismondi for making such a historically informed, important, empowering, and totally relevant film. See it today!

© **Jan Lisa Huttner (3/19/10)—Special for WomenArts**

The Soloist
Directed by Joe Wright
Screenplay by Susannah Grant
(Based on columns by Steve Lopez)

Principal Actors: Robert Downey, Jr. & Jamie Foxx

Always on the prowl for human interest stories, reporter "Steve Lopez" (played by Robert Downey, Jr.) meets a homeless man named "Nathaniel Ayers" (played by Jamie Foxx). Although the relationship begins on a professional level, Steve finds himself inexorably drawn into the grim details of Nathaniel's troubled life.

Jamie Foxx conveys a wide range of emotions as Nathaniel, but good as he is, the point-of-view in The Soloist *is always Steve's, and this may well be the deepest, most sincere performance Robert Downey, Jr. has ever given. "Uplift" is elusive in this painful film (loosely based on columns written by a real reporter), but Susannah Grant's screenplay demonstrates that the only thing worse than struggling and suffering is giving up and giving in.*

Penny's Points: ✳✳✳✳

In February 1899, decades before she became the first American woman to win a Nobel Peace Prize, Jane Addams wrote a heartfelt essay for *The Atlantic* magazine called "The Subtle Problems with Charity."

> "Many of the difficulties in philanthropy come from an unconscious division of the world into the philanthropists and those to be helped," Addams begins. "Of the various struggles which a decade of residence in [the Hull-House] settlement implies, none have made a more definite impression on my mind than the incredibly painful difficulties which involve both giver and recipient when one person asks charitable aid of another."

There is no "peace of mind," she concludes, after many examples of fractious misunderstandings, only "pangs and misgivings." So why even try? Because the only thing worse than doing the wrong thing is doing nothing.

Audience members, be warned: If you're looking for "uplift" from the new film *The Soloist,* then stay away. After struggling and suffering, characters filled with "pangs and misgivings" find themselves facing more struggling and more suffering. So why keep trying when there is no redemption? The only thing worse than struggling and suffering is giving up and giving in.

The Soloist begins when a reporter named "Steve Lopez" (Robert Downey, Jr.) meets a homeless man named "Nathaniel Ayers" (Jamie Foxx). Steve writes a column, so he's always on the prowl for human interest stories, and something about Nathaniel piques his curiosity. He does some research and submits his copy, and soon one "Nathaniel column" leads to another, drawing Steve inexorably into the grim details of Nathaniel's troubled life.

Steve's "Nathaniel columns" bring him awards and accolades, but at some point he inadvertently crosses a professional boundary between reporter and source. He has transformed Nathaniel into a local media personality, so what next? Is he now Nathaniel's "keeper," his friend, what?

Jamie Foxx conveys a wide range of emotions as Nathaniel. He never condescends, but he also never lets us forget that this man is deeply disturbed. Nathaniel will never be capable of conventional relationships, but his ability to love others begins to manifest itself when he starts allowing others to love him, first Steve and then his sister "Jennifer" (played by Lisagay Hamilton). Nevertheless, their love for him will always be mixed with fear, fear of his emotional storms and physical explosions, fear of his vulnerability and fragile hold on activities of daily living that most of us take for granted.

Good as Foxx is, the point-of-view in *The Soloist* is always Steve's, and Robert Downey, Jr. is terrific. Downey brings all of his own anguish to Steve, wearing his life experiences as the glasses through which he looks out at Nathaniel's world. We all know Downey's back story, his years of addiction and imprisonment, and when he spends the night with Nathaniel on Skid Row, his empathy is palpable. This may well be the deepest, most sincere performance he's ever given.

In numerous interviews, screenwriter Susannah Grant says she started interviewing both Steve and Nathaniel while Steve was writing his book *(The Soloist: A Lost Dream, an Unlikely Friendship, and the Redemptive Power of Music)*. In other words, the book and the screenplay developed in parallel, so the screenplay is not "based on" the book in any direct sense. As an accomplished screenwriter (best known for her Oscar-nominated *Erin Brockovich* screenplay), Grant always focuses on telling her story even when the characters she creates to fit it diverge from the facts at hand.

The Steve Lopez character that results is the polar opposite of the cinematic Erin Brockovich (also a real person transformed into a Hollywood heroine). The Brockovich character was a crusader, convinced of her mission and willing to do whatever was required to achieve it. The Lopez character is anguished and filled with foreboding; even knowing he has the best of intentions, Steve is never sure of how to use the power he has acquired over Nathaniel's life.

The relationships Grant develops for this Lopez "character" amplify his uncertainty. This is not a documentary, so the actual facts of Lopez's life are irrelevant. Is "the real Steve Lopez" happily married? Is he a great father who has solid relationships with all his kids? Don't know. Don't care. This film is about the emotional changes that occur when a man of status and privilege bonds with a man with neither, and Grant has found powerful ways to convey his transformation.

Despite huge hype and multiple Oscar nominations, I was personally underwhelmed by both of director Joe Wright's prior films, *Pride & Prejudice* (2005) and *Atonement* (2007), so I did not have high hopes when I walked into the theater to see *The Soloist*. But Wright stays in the background this time and serves the story. Perhaps he was humbled, like the real Steve Lopez evidently was, by the responsibility entailed in trying to tell it. Based on all the manipulative previews I saw in advance, I did not expect to be so moved by this film, but I was, and it has stayed with me for days.

© **Jan Lisa Huttner (5/7/09)—Special for WomenArts**

Sunshine Cleaning
Directed by Christine Jeffs
Screenplay by Megan Holley

Principal Actors: Amy Adams
with Emily Blunt & Alan Arkin

News flash: houses don't clean themselves! Although Sunshine Cleaning *resembles 2007 Oscar-winner* Little Miss Sunshine *in several superficial ways, don't let the coincidental "sunshine" reference blind you. Writer Megan Holley built her original screenplay around a story she heard eight years ago on National Public Radio—two women describing the trials and tribulations of running their own crime scene clean-up business. In* Sunshine Cleaning, *these friends become sisters Rose and Norah Lorkowski.*

We're culturally conditioned to believe that women who function as homemakers and caregivers aren't interesting. For all the rhetoric about "motherhood and apple pie," the work women do to maintain their households is usually trivialized and economically exploited. But Jeffs and Holley both understand there is genuine satisfaction to be derived from setting things aright (even knowing new messes await us tomorrow), and they move their story along with just the right mix of giggles and gross-outs.

Penny's Points: ✳✳✳✳

News flash: houses don't clean themselves! Yes, many activities of daily living have changed since the first Neanderthals left their caves, but human effort is still required to work all our labor saving devices. And even though many 21st century men now do tasks their ancestors would have found humiliating, housekeeping has always been "women's work" and likely always will be. In her new film *Sunshine Cleaning*, director Christine Jeffs takes ownership of these historical truths to great effect.

Although *Sunshine Cleaning* resembles 2007 Oscar-winner *Little Miss Sunshine* in several superficial ways, don't let the coincidental "sunshine" reference blind you. These two films have totally different storylines and fundamentally different aims. While most of the characters in *Little Miss Sunshine* want to "be somebody," ambition is never a primary motivator in *Sunshine Cleaning*. Alternatives like suicide and addictive oblivion are essential plot elements, so when characters in *Sunshine Cleaning* decide to keep on keeping on, they're fully aware of the option to give up and stop trying. But one thing *Little Miss Sunshine* and *Sunshine Cleaning* definitely do have in common: they're both dramedies which depict real life dilemmas with warmth and comic flair.

Writer Megan Holley built her original screenplay around a story she heard one day on National Public Radio—two women describing the trials and tribulations of running their own crime scene clean-up business. In *Sunshine Cleaning* these friends become sisters: "Rose" (Amy Adams) and "Norah" (Emily Blunt) Lorkowski. Their mother died when the girls were youngsters, so Rose, the older sister, just took over, thereby setting up a pattern of mutual dependence bristling with resentment and hostility on both sides. Their father, "Joe" (Alan Arkin), tries to mediate in little ways, but mostly he keeps to himself, determined to stay out of their way.

When the film opens, Rose is working for a residential cleaning service. Her uniform is a pink tee shirt with the logo "Pretty Clean" above her right breast. Meanwhile Norah is waitressing in a tiny hamburger joint too small and too transient for uniforms. Rose is embroiled in a long, sad affair with a married cop named "Mac" (Steve Zahn) who is probably the father of her son "Oscar" (Jason Spevack), although Mac and Oscar never have any direct onscreen contact. Rose needs money, so Mac offers to recommend her for crime scene clean-up jobs. She's cleaning up other people's messes anyway, so why not get paid by an insurance company?

First time out, Rose has no idea what she's doing, and Norah, dragged along like usual, knows even less, but gradually their new jobs take hold. Used to working in beautiful homes that can never be hers, Rose enjoys stepping into extreme situations and making things better, while Norah gets a buzz from her sudden proximity to other people's intimate secrets. The money may not be much, but it's definitely more, and soon Rose is reading manuals and registering for licensing exams, with Norah, Joe, and Oscar all feeding off her energy and resolve.

If you concede that Batman, Ironman, Spiderman and their multitudinous superhero friends all travel along parallel arcs, then I'll concede that Rose and Norah resemble the lead characters in *27 Dresses, Blue Crush, In Her Shoes,* and other films about girls who grow up without a nurturing maternal presence. For the best example, look with new eyes at Barbra Streisand's film *Yentl* (recently re-released in a 2-disk 25th anniversary DVD box set). In both films, single fathers foist domestic responsibilities on their daughters when they're way too young to cope. Nevertheless the heroines in both films eventually surprise themselves by finding genuine satisfaction in care-giving.

We're culturally conditioned to believe that women who function as homemakers and caregivers aren't interesting. For all the rhetoric about "motherhood and apple pie," the work women do to maintain their households is usually trivialized and economically exploited. So it's great to see a film that takes domesticity seriously without evasion or apology. Jeffs and Holley both understand there is genuine satisfaction to be derived from setting things aright (even knowing new messes await us tomorrow), and they move their story along with just the right mix of giggles and gross-outs.

Sunshine Cleaning is also blessed with two excellent lead actresses. Amy Adams provides most of the heart as Rose and Emily Blunt provides most of the humor as Norah, but both characters are complex and both arcs are illuminating. Adams has a lovely inner light that glows ever more brightly with each new bit of hard-won self-acceptance. Blunt is particularly good at slowly peeling back Norah's defenses to reveal her soft side, and she shares some of her best scenes with Mary Lynn Rajskub (playing one victim's abandoned daughter).

There are men in this story too, of course, but they're all supporting characters. To their great credit, Jeffs and Holley refuse to distract us with romantic entanglements. (I remember being baffled by reviews of *Under the Tuscan Sun* that focused on the brief affair between Diane Lane and Raoul Bova. The film I saw was a love story about a woman and her house!)

Sunshine Cleaning is a film that everyone should see. I hope it's still playing on Mother's Day. What a perfect (and gently didactic) family outing!

© **Jan Lisa Huttner (4/9/09)—Special for WomenArts**

The Tempest
Written & Directed by Julie Taymor
(Based on a play by William Shakespeare)

Principal Actors: Helen Mirren
with Djimon Hounsou & Ben Whishaw

Julie Taymor's new adaptation of The Tempest *is a marvel of sight and sound! First performed in 1611, William Shakespeare's final play is the culmination of both life wisdom and theatrical craft. The focus of Shakespeare's drama is a wizard named Prospero. Once the ruler of Milan, Prospero was deposed by his brother, set adrift, and washed up on an enchanted island. Years later, watching from a high cliff as his enemies sail into view, Prospero sees his opportunity for revenge.*

But in Taymor's hands Shakespeare's fundamentally masculine plot is revitalized with a deeply feminine sensibility. She changes Prospero into "Prospera" (played by Helen Mirren at her most magnificent and multifaceted), and thereby forces us to reexamine all our assumptions about motivation and narrative drive.

Penny's Points: ✳✳✳✳

Julie Taymor's new adaptation of *The Tempest* is a marvel of sight and sound!

First performed in 1611, William Shakespeare's final play is the culmination of both life wisdom and theatrical craft. Four hundred years later, the language may be arcane but the emotions (passion and grief, betrayal and revenge) are as deep, resonant, and immediately recognizable as the day they were first penned. And in Taymor's hands Shakespeare's fundamentally masculine plot is revitalized with a deeply feminine sensibility.

The focus of Shakespeare's drama is a wizard named Prospero. Once the ruler of Milan, Prospero was deposed by his brother Antonio and set adrift in a small boat with his tiny daughter Miranda (the original play's only female cast member). Miraculously they survived, and now, after a dozen years spent on an enchanted island, Prospero sees his opportunity for revenge when Antonio sails past, returning home after attending a royal wedding in Tunis. Prospero creates a wild storm (the tempest of the title) which tosses the ship's inhabitants into the sea. Then he sprinkles them onto separate beaches—dazed and disoriented, but very much alive.

Three days after the storm, Prospero reveals himself to his "guests" (all of whom have been fully tested by their travails in the interim), and together they all sail back to Italy. The film's action (like the play's), revolves around the adventures of the shipwrecked men, driven forward at Prospero's command.

Shakespeare braided his plot with three strands: first Prospero's brother Antonio in the company of his lord King Alonso (also attended by his advisor Gonzalo and his brother Sebastian); next Alonso's butler Stephano (carried ashore on a barrel of wine) and Trinculo (the court jester); and finally Prince

Ferdinand (Alonso's son) who believes that he is the wreck's sole survivor.

For four hundred years, scholars have focused on the parallel between Shakespeare and Prospero: two conjurers holding their captive audiences in thrall. Then along comes Taymor, who changes Prospero into "Prospera" (Helen Mirren at her most magnificent and multifaceted), and thereby forces us to reexamine all our assumptions about motivation and narrative drive.

Shakespeare's hero, a man wronged, wants to be restored to his former position. Taymor's heroine, equally wronged, is also acutely aware of the need to secure a future for her daughter "Miranda" (played by sweet-faced Felicity Jones) while she still has the power to do so.

In Shakespeare's original, the island is populated by natives (described as "strange Shapes" when they appear before Alonso and his retinue in Act Three and as "Spirits, Nymphs and Reapers" when Prospero summons them in Act Four), but Taymor has stripped everyone extraneous from the plot in order to focus on just two: incorporeal "Ariel" played by Ben Whishaw (who starred last year as ethereal poet John Keats in *Bright Star*) and earthy "Caliban" played by Djimon Hounsou (who made an unforgettable debut in *Amistad* and received an Oscar nomination a few years back for his commanding role in *Blood Diamond*).

When we first meet them, Ariel has a privileged position in Prospera's world. She calls him "dainty Ariel," "delicate Ariel," and "my bird," and she treats him like a treasured pet. In contrast, she calls Caliban "my slave," and treats him accordingly.

Ariel became Prospera's servant when she freed him from a tree, and everything she knows about the island's history she knows from him. According to Ariel, his tormenter was "the foul witch Sycorax," a woman brought to the island and left there years before. As Ariel tells it, the pretext for her banishment from Algiers was also witchcraft, but Prospera refuses to see any parallel between Sycorax's "mischiefs manifold and sorceries terrible" and her own "secret studies."

Caliban is Sycorax's son. Pregnant when she was forced from her home in Algiers, she gave birth and died sometime later. Arriving from Milan after Sycorax's death, Prospera took pity on the orphan boy. She taught him culture, language, and religion; Caliban, in exchange, showed Prospera the island's "fresh springs" and "fertile places." Prospera's daughter and Sycorax's son were the only human children on the island, and she raised them together until the years passed and Caliban's thoroughly human and totally predictable longing for Miranda (now grown into a beautiful teenager) filled Prospera with rage. And thus did Caliban, in Taymor's telling of Shakespeare's tale, becomes the agent of Prospera's awakening.

As a woman, Prospera understands that, having no other human choices available to her, Miranda will eventually give herself to Caliban, and thereby wed herself to the island forever. And so, for Miranda's sake, Taymor's Prospera renounces revenge, choosing to save Alonso and all his retinue (including the hateful Antonio) so that Miranda can have a future. From the moment Prospera, watching from a high cliff, sees her enemies sail into view, lessons must be learned before the various characters (including Prospera herself) can be released, newly cleansed, back to Western civilization.

This is William Shakespeare's story brought vividly to life by Julie Taymor. In addition to Mirren, Jones, Hounsou, and Whishaw, her perfect cast includes Russell Brand as "Trinculo" (the jester), Reese Carney as "Prince Ferdinand" (King Alonso's son), Alan Cumming as "Sebastian" (King Alonso's brother), Tom Conti as "Gonzalo" (King Alonso's advisor), Chris

Cooper as "Antonio," (Prospera's brother), Alfred Molina as "Stephano" (King Alonso's butler), and David Strathairn as "King Alonso."

Taymor's wonderful technical crew is lead by cinematographer Stuart Dryburgh (nominated for an Oscar for his work on Jane Campion's masterpiece *The Piano*), costume designer Sandy Powell (winner of Oscars for *Shakespeare in Love* and *The Young Victoria*), and composer Elliot Goldenthal (Oscar-winner for the score he wrote for Taymor's film *Frida*).

The special effects required to depict Whishaw as an "airy sprite" are simple, low tech, and highly effective. And Goldenthal composed lovely music for Whishaw so he could sing the poems Shakespeare wrote for Ariel in verse. All these artists make glorious individual contributions to *The Tempest*, augmenting Hawaii's naturally cinematic coastline.

Stimulating to the mind, intoxicating to the senses, how can there be no place for Julie Taymor's version of *The Tempest* on this year's list of likely Oscar nominees? And yet, three weeks after it opened "in limited release," it's only being shown on thirteen screens in the entire USA. Here in Chicago, it's only offered on one screen, and only for one show per day!

Alas, no one seems to care much anymore about this "brave new world that has such people in it." So unfortunately most of you will have to wait for the DVD :-(

© **Jan Lisa Huttner (12/27/10)—Special for WomenArts**

CHAPTER FOUR
3.5 POINTS

"The whole is **less** than the sum of its parts."

The Kids Are All Right
Directed by Lisa Cholodenko
Screenplay by Cholodenko & Stuart Blumberg

Principal Actors: Julianne Moore
with Annette Bening & Mark Ruffalo

Teenagers "Joni" (Mia Wasikowska) and "Laser" (Josh Hutcherson) are half-siblings raised by lesbian couple "Jules" (Julianne Moore) and "Nic" (Annette Bening) who used the sperm of a single donor. Joni's just about to leave for college, but before she goes Laser convinces her to help him track down their bio-Dad. Joni's call comes totally out of the blue, nevertheless "Paul" (Mark Ruffalo) immediately agrees to meet with them. The first half of The Kids Are All Right *is delightfully funny. The characters have their individual quirks, but they're all sympathetic and engaging, and the casting is perfect. Then it all goes wrong, spinning from family dramedy into sex-farce before collapsing into a politically-correct message movie that literally ends in a big group hug.*

Penny's Points: ✳✳✳½

I really, really wanted to like this film. I'm a big fan of *High Art* (writer/director Lisa Cholodenko's first film), and I liked her second film *(Laurel Canyon)* too, so I was excited when I heard she was about to release a new film. But now that I've seen it, pondered awhile, and seen it again, I just have to bite the bullet and face facts: *The Kids Are All Right* just doesn't work for me.

It's summertime in southern California, and teenage "Joni" (Mia Wasikowska) is getting ready to start college. This is a traumatic rite of passage for all nuclear families, but Joni's family structure makes for additional complications. Her younger brother "Laser" (Josh Hutcherson) is actually her half-brother, and they've been raised by a lesbian couple they refer to as "the Moms." "Nic" (Annette Bening) is their ambitious, perfectionist, breadwinning Mom, and "Jules" (Julianne Moore) is their docile, nurturing, homemaking Mom.

Anxious about life without Joni home to buffer, Laser asks her to track down their bio-Dad. Since Joni is already 18, she's legally empowered to contact the sperm bank; at 15, Laser is at her mercy. Joni is surprised and reluctant ("This will hurt Moms' feelings."), but the urgency of his plea ("I've never asked you for anything before.") weighs on her conscience, so Joni makes the call.

Cut to "Paul" (Mark Ruffalo), the owner of a trendy local restaurant for which he personally grows produce on an urban mini-farm. His life is full of wine, women, sex, and sun, but when the sperm bank calls, he says sure, fine, no problem, and in the blink of an eye, Paul finds himself face-to-face with two teenagers in search of a father figure.

The first half of *The Kids Are All Right* is delightfully funny. The set-up is loose and easy; the pace is sharp and quick. The characters have their individual quirks, but they're all sympathetic and engaging, and the casting is perfect.

Wasikowska looks a lot like Bening and captures many of her mannerisms, but she also has a natural physical rapport with Ruffalo. Hutcherson looks a lot like Ruffalo, but he also embodies Moore's inner glow. Then it all goes wrong, spinning from family dramedy into sex-farce before collapsing into a politically-correct message movie that literally ends in a big group hug.

I see lots and lots of films every year (upwards of 300), so I'm used to leaving theatres disappointed, but in this case I'm genuinely distressed. I'm sure Cholodenko's primary goal was to tell a good story. (As my husband/partner Richard always says: "No one ever tries to make a bad movie.") But I suspect she also wanted to make a commercially successful movie, and that's an uphill battle for all women filmmakers these days, especially lesbians who want to work from their own experience.

Cholodenko worked alone on her first two films, but *Kids* has a co-writer, Stuart Blumberg, whose main claim to fame is a romantic triangle comedy called *Keeping the Faith*. (Will it jog your memory if I say it stars Jena Elfman, Edward Norton, and Ben Stiller? And if I remind you that Norton plays a Catholic priest and Stiller plays his Jewish buddy? Nope, didn't think so.). Blumberg's not to blame for what ensues; Cholodenko clearly wanted the input of an experienced male RomCom writer, and that's exactly what she got.

The big loser is Annette Bening. While Jules and Paul are bouncing around his bedroom, Nic's stuck at home... drinking heavily, becoming shrill, and turning pathetic. What if Cholodenko and Blumberg had added a work-based scene for her? What if they had given Nic a chance to vent about Joni's imminent departure and the destabilizing effect it was having on her family? We'll never know. As it is, Cholodenko and Blumberg set Bening up with a raw, painful dinner party scene, and she hits the ball out of the park, but this boffo performance by an A-List actress occurs too late to redeem her character.

Focus Features is devoting a lot of resources to the *Kids* marketing campaign, and they've embarked on a sophisticated roll-out strategy that seems to have worked well for recently successful Indies like *Garden State* and *Little Miss Sunshine*. I wish them all best because I'd really like to see more Lisa Cholodenko films in future. So go with moderate expectations and you might well have a fine time.

SPOILER ALERT!!!
Please do not read until after you've seen *The Kids Are All Right*

There's one specific moment in *Kids* when the whole film curdled and turned sour for me. Jules decides to enter the landscaping business and she hires a Hispanic gardener to help with the heavy lifting. Jules has no clients and no references, but Paul hires her to redo his huge multilevel backyard anyway. (Question: Nic is a physician, so her family's lifestyle is based on a solid professional income, but where is Paul getting all his money???)

So anyway, there's Jules in Paul's garden, bent over, thong exposed, digging in the fragrant earth. And there's "Luis" (Joaquin Garrido) watching as Paul drools from above, the lord on his balcony surveying his domain. But we're still in comedy mode, so the audience is encouraged to laugh right along with Luis, and laugh we do, right up to the moment Jules fires him.

This is a film that wants us all to applaud alternative lifestyles, but then uses its only Hispanic character as a totally dispensable comic scapegoat. There's also one Asian character (male) and one African American character (female) that get the same short shrift. So me, I had a hard time smiling when all those LA Anglos were hugging each other at the very end.

© **Jan Lisa Huttner (7/9/10)—Special for WomenArts**

The Women
Written & Directed by Diane English
(Based on characters originally created
by Clare Boothe Luce in 1936)

Principal Actors: Meg Ryan
with Annette Bening & Candice Bergen

Fortysomething years of frenetic activity come to a screeching halt one day when "Mary Haines" (Meg Ryan) inadvertently learns that her husband Stephen is having an affair. Retreating from men, Mary reaches out to an already large and rapidly expanding support network. Old friends offer advice, and new friends provide consolation, but in the end Mary comes to see herself anew as the daughter of her mother and the mother of her daughter. Writer/Director Diane English and her megawatt cast transform an estrogen-rich confection from a cold satire into a warm dramedy.

Penny's Points: ✳✳✳½

Diane English's new adaptation of the Depression-era classic *The Women* is a huge ensemble piece with megawatt star power; counting up the Oscar, Emmy, and Golden Globe nominations of all the cast members would likely take hours. Skinny cappuccino in hand, I settled into my seat in the Chicago screening room, more than happy to just sit back for 114 minutes and watch these ladies strut their stuff.

The plot of *The Women* swirls around the character of "Mary Haines" (Meg Ryan), a carefully raised girl from a wealthy family. When the story begins, she's reached the middle of her life, as if flown in on a magic carpet. She has soared above all pain and privation, convinced that she is now artfully balancing all expectations: daughter, wife, mother, friend, employer, society hostess, clothing designer – is there anything Mary can't do? Obviously Humpty Dumpty sits poised on the wall, just about to have her big fall!

Fortysomething years of frenetic activity come to a screeching halt once Mary inadvertently learns that her husband Stephen is having an affair with a gorgeous woman selling luxury perfumes at the Saks flagship store on Fifth Avenue. Thinking back on all the late nights at the office, the sudden cancellation of a long-planned vacation, etc, Mary realizes that her husband had long since disengaged, but she just wasn't ready to face it.

Then another crisis: her father calls, and she walks straight into a second buzz saw. Of course she's furious, but she hates herself just as much as she hates them. Betrayed by the two most important men in her life, the two men who previously protected her both emotionally and financially from all mundane concerns, Mary starts asking herself all the questions she's always avoided, starting with the most obvious two: "Who am I?" and "What do I want out of life?"

Retreating from men, Mary reaches out to an already large and rapidly expanding support network. Old friends offer advice, and new friends provide consolation. BFF "Sylvie" (Annette Bening), an ambitious magazine publisher, urges aggressive counterattack. "Leah" (Bette Midler), a fellow-sufferer at a New Age retreat, supplies bemused detachment. Back on the home front, housekeeper "Maggie" (Cloris Leachman) stays loyal to Mary, commenting on the action even as she prepares her own escape plan. (Will divorce exhaust the Haines' financial resources?)

Carrie Fisher, Joanna Gleason, Eva Mendes, Debi Mazar, Debra Messing, Jada Pinkett Smith, and Lynn Whitfield—beloved actresses all—parade across the screen. And they each get well-balanced scenes and nicely defined arcs, even though many of their parts, by necessity, are quite small. (Note that *The Women* has an all-female cast with no male speaking parts.) But in the end, the most touching moments in *The Women* are firmly grounded in Mary's two most primal relationships: with her mother "Catherine" (Candice Bergen) and her daughter "Molly" (India Ennenga).

Whereas most "prick flicks" focus on superheroes endowed with extraordinary powers, most "chick flicks" are about real women trying to lead balanced lives. *The Women* literally asks us to walk in a few new pairs of shoes for a bit, and just to make sure we get it, when we walk through Saks with Syvie, her designer sunglasses feed us data (as if she were Arnold Schwarzenegger's "Terminator" searching for Sarah Connor). A few scenes later, Sylvie gives these same glasses to Molly. Get it? English is daring us to trivialize the very real joys and sorrows of Mary's life just because she has a lovely home in Connecticut! By what right, she asks, do filmmakers elevate mayhem above the mundane?

With all the hoopla surrounding the huge success of *Sex and the City* earlier this summer, it's inevitable that most critics will compare these two films. But while Mary's gal pals are a crucial component of her psychic equilibrium (thereby making *SATC* a legitimate source for comparison), I think *The Women* is after something very different. As the narrative unfolds, Mary has occasion to see herself anew as the daughter of her mother and the mother of her daughter. What has she learned from her mother? What is she teaching her daughter? Transforming an estrogen-rich confection from a cold satire into a warm dramedy, English and her cast help us see that, in the end, these are the two questions by which this Mary Haines will ultimately judge her own life.

Bottom line: I laughed (a lot), I cried (a little), and then I tossed my empty cup and left the screening room with a smile.

SPOILER ALERT!!!
Please do NOT read until AFTER you have seen *The Women*

Truth be told, I've never been a great fan of Clare Boothe Luce's version of *The Women*. I can't say exactly when I first saw George Cukor's first film adaption from 1939 (starring Norma Shearer as "Mrs. Stephen Haines," with back-up from another stellar cast including Joan Crawford, Joan Fontaine, Paulette Goddard, Marjorie Main, and Rosalind Russell), but I saw it several times long ago, and I recently saw a revival of the original stage version from 1936 (starring Cynthia Nixon as "Mary"). So I went into Diane English's version curious to see how she would update something I definitely consider "a period piece." (For example: what to do with the dude ranch? Oy!)

A few facts about Clare Boothe Luce from her *New York Times* obit (written by Albin Krebs and published on October 10, 1987):

"Clare Boothe was born in New York City on April 10, 1903, the daughter of William Franklin Boothe, a pit orchestra violinist and sometime businessman, and the former Anna Clara Snyder, who had been a chorus girl... Her parents separated when Clare was eight years old. She was brought up in genteel poverty by her mother...

In 1919, her mother married Dr. Albert Elmer Austin, a prominent physician in Greenwich, Conn... In church, Clare Boothe met her future husband: George Tuttle Brokaw, millionaire-playboy son of a clothing manufacturer. They married in 1923 in a wedding called 'the most important social event of the season.' It was not to last. Mr. Brokaw, 23 years older than his bride, was a heavy drinker, according to one of his biographers, and he was prone to abuse his wife. After six years of marriage she won a divorce on the grounds of mental cruelty... Declining to rest on her money, Clare Boothe importuned a society friend, Conde Nast, publisher of *Vogue* and *Vanity Fair,* for a job... She became managing editor [of *Vanity Fair*]... She left in 1934."

A few subsequent details from Wikipedia: She married Henry Luce, founder and publisher of *Time* magazine on November 23, 1935. The original Broadway production of *The Women* opened on December 26, 1936, and even though it was received "coolly by critics," "it was "immensely popular with the public," running for 657 performances. By the time of her death in 1987, Clare Boothe Luce had added war correspondent, Congresswoman, and Ambassador to her astonishing list of accomplishments.

So without dwelling on psychobiography, let's just say Clare Boothe Luce had plenty of reasons to distrust men, nevertheless achieving a level of success that left her mother's considerable skills as a social climber in the dust. Although most people see satire when they watch original versions of *The Women,* I see Clare Boothe Luce's gritty determination to carve her own destiny, coupled with the self-disgust that resulted from doing what she had to do to get where she wanted to go. The bitter aftertaste always leeches through the frothy surface.

*****

Most of the characters in the '08 version have 36/39 counterparts, but in each case their personalities are extremely different. The most significant change transforms Rosalind Russell's "Sylvia" into Annette Bening's "Sylvie." While these two characters perform many of the same plot functions, Sylvia is just a gossipy bitch whereas Sylvie is literally tangled up in good intentions. Sylvie's reward is her relationship with Molly (which creates the opportunity for her eventual reconciliation with Mary). Sylvia's arc ends in ostracism and marital misery.

Mary's mother and daughter are both minor characters in the original. The name "Molly" is new; in 1939, actress Virginia Weidler was called "Little Mary." The name "Catherine" is also new; in 1939, actress Lucile Watson was simply called "Mrs. Moorehead."

There was absolutely no relationship between Sylvia and Little Mary in '36 or '39, and I think adding one in the '08 version is a very nice touch.

In '36 and '39, Crystal marries Stephen and then has an affair with one of the other husbands, making her not just a bitch but a tramp. This original Crystal came of age in the middle of the Great Depression, so many women in the audience would have admired her ferocious survival skills, even while applauding her comeuppance. Although he's never given the chance to speak for himself, the Stephen of 36/39 presumably comes crawling back to Mary after Crystal publically humiliates him. When they remarry, setting their social world right again, neither will ever acknowledge what they both surely know: Stephen is the one who's lost the most face in their set.

In '08, Crystal and Stephen start living together, but they never marry and Crystal has no additional entanglements. The '08 Stephen wants to come home because life with Crystal is boring. Stephen is an ambitious man, and Mary seduces him anew with the big buzz surrounding her new company—the company financed by Catherine.

Do I need to say no women of color played significant roles in the '39 version? How wonderful to have self-possessed characters like those played by Eva Mendes, Jada Pinkett Smith, and Lynn Whitfield now! On the other hand, I love the fact that two Jewish women play transformative figures in both depictions of this mostly WASP-world. Paulette Goddard was "Miriam Aarons" in '39, and Bette Midler is "Leah Miller" in '08. Besides giving her an easily decoded name, there's nothing especially Jewish about "Miriam Aarons," but I like the fact that English honored this element.

Finally: the fashion show!!! George Cukor's 1939 version of *The Women* was filmed in lustrous black and white, but midway through there's a Technicolor fashion show!!! Just like when Dorothy wakes up to find herself in Munchkinland!!! (Yup, *The Wizard of Oz* was also released in 1939.)

Maybe there really were women in 1939 with sufficient cash and courage to both buy and wear these clothes. Probably some women now buy and wear the things they see on *SATC* (or knock-offs thereof). Frankly, Carrie's outfits have always repelled me. Since I'm no fashionista, maybe this is a bad sign, but I would happily wear several of the items in Mary's new collection. If this film is a box office success, maybe I'll even get that option!

© **Jan Lisa Huttner (9/13/08)–Special for WomenArts**

Waitress
Written and Directed by Adrienne Shelly

Principal Actors: Keri Russell
with Nathan Fillion & Jeremy Sisto

Shelly wrote Waitress *when she was carrying her first child, and the birth of her daughter Sophie served to liberate her voice rather than stifle it. Newsweek quotes* Waitress *producer Michael Roiff remembering the day Shelly proudly crowed: "See, it CAN be done!" (referencing her accomplishments as a working mother). Entering Jenna's world did not come naturally to me, but once I relaxed into it, I was thoroughly charmed. Keri Russell does a terrific job as Jenna, capturing complex, layered emotions in every single scene. The best parts take place in a diner called Joe's Pie Shop, where Jenna works side by side with "Dawn" and "Becky." Like all true workplace buddies, Becky, Jenna and Dawn are totally interdependent and indispensable to one another for as long as they need to be.*

Penny's Points: ✳✳✳½

In the 2003 IFC documentary *In the Company of Women,* actress Tilda Swinton talks frankly about why she thinks men should see films about women: "It's a very rare holiday still to be given the opportunity to go into a woman's psyche, and see the world, and see the existential experience of life through her eyes." The new film *Waitress,* written and directed by Adrienne Shelly, is precisely this kind of holiday. Everything we know about this waitress ("Jenna"), we know from the inside, and what little we know about her world comes from her perspective.

Jenna is no realist; retreating ever further from the world after the death of her mother, she sees herself as the heroine of a fairy tale. Her odious husband "Earl" (Jeremy Sisto) is a good looking guy who must have seemed like Prince Charming once, but in a reversal of fairy tale conventions, the more she kisses him, the more she sees he's a frog. Every day, Earl finds occasion to remind Jenna that her seemingly comfortable home is in fact his castle.

Instead of spinning straw into gold like the miller's daughter in Rumpelstiltskin, Jenna makes pies. If Alison Anders, the filmmaker behind the waitress-centered indie *Gas, Food, Lodging*, had directed this film, Jenna would be living on the edge of exhaustion. One person cannot possibly make all these pies, from scratch yet, especially when she's also responsible for serving them. But fairy tales don't tackle grim truths head on; Shelly's candy-colored palette is enough to convince us, all by itself and right from the start, that Jenna's story is heading towards a suitably happy ending.

There is no way to turn back the clock. By the time you read this review, you will probably know that Adrienne Shelly was murdered in her Manhattan office last November. I certainly knew this awful fact when I saw *Waitress* at a critics screening in Chicago last month. So maybe one day it will be possible to see this film "in itself," but for right now, we must deal with it in context.

In context, then, *Waitress* will open in New York and LA on the heels of yet another New York Times article in which dismal new "Celluloid Ceiling" statistics are attributed to the fact that women aren't really committed to careers. Ignoring everything else that her other sources tell her, Sharon Waxman concludes with this quote from retired producer Sherry Lansing: "Women [also] want to be in love. A huge percentage want children. They want friends. They want life." ["Hollywood's Shortage of Female Power;" April 26, 2007]

But Shelly's legacy points us in the opposite direction: in both her own brief life and in the life of her character Jenna, fulfillment comes through the combination. Being a director was an opportunity to "nurture people." Acting as a leader was "a really sexy feeling." Shelly wrote *Waitress* when she was carrying her first child, and the birth of her daughter Sophie served to liberate her voice rather than stifle it. Newsweek quotes *Waitress* producer Michael Roiff remembering the day Shelly proudly crowed: "See, it CAN be done!" (referencing her accomplishments as a working mother).

Sitting in the screening room last month, I was filled with emotion. I'm not a girly-girl and none of my close friends are either, so entering Jenna's world did not come naturally to me. But once I relaxed into it, I was thoroughly charmed. Keri Russell does a terrific job as Jenna, capturing complex, layered emotions in every single scene. The best parts take place in a diner called Joe's Pie Shop, where Jenna works side by side with Dawn and Becky. Like all true workplace buddies, Becky, Jenna and Dawn are totally interdependent and indispensable to one another for as long as they need to be. As is often the case when women bond, the fact that they would probably never be friends if they hadn't landed in the same place at the same time is totally irrelevant. Shelly cast herself as "Dawn," a sweetly quirky klutz; her counterweight is brash, tough-talking "Becky" (expertly played by Cheryl Hines).

The male roles in *Waitress* are less interesting. Lew Temple as "Cal", the manager, is a paper tiger; Andy Griffith, playing the old coot customer, is a bit too obvious; and Nathan Fillion as "Dr. Pomatter", the handsome new guy in town, is too good to be true, even in a fairy tale. But Jeremy Sisto is truly chilling as

Earl. Like Woody Harellson in last year's excellent adaptation *The Prize Winner of Defiance, Ohio,* he somehow convinced me to feel sorry for him even as I wanted to kill him on Jenna's behalf.

Given the media hype surrounding her tragic death, *Waitress* has a chance to be a box office success (unlike, say *Prize Winner* which definitely deserved better). I will never have the chance to meet Shelly face-to-face, so I will never know for sure, but I'm guessing she would appreciate the irony. Here's her answer to the "Celluloid Ceiling" question (from *In the Company of Women*):

"It's funny; I've come full circle on this topic. I started out saying: 'I'm never, ever going to speak like it's harder because I'm a woman. That's the last thing I'm ever, ever gonna do.' And then, five years later, I was saying: 'You know, it really is much harder because I'm a woman, much harder, and I want everyone to know and I want to talk about it constantly.' And then, now, I'm sorta back to feeling like it's hard for everybody. It's hard. It's a hard business."

For her family and friends there can be no consolation, but those of us who will only know Adrienne Shelly by her work can still hope that the story of *Waitress* has a suitably happy ending.

© **Jan Lisa Huttner (5/1/07)—Special for Digital Filmmaker**

APPENDIX

10 Years in the Pond:
From Lonely Ducklings to a Bevy of Swans

2002: Sparks ignited on the morning of June 2, 2002 when Chicago writer Jan Lisa Huttner (longtime member of the American Association of University Women) read an article in the Sunday *New York Times* about the "Celluloid Ceiling." The article, quoting statistics by Communications Professor Martha Lauzen of San Diego State University, compelled Huttner to take action. She wrote a letter to the *Times,* they published it, and a new cause took root.

2003: Working with Program Vice President Linda Henning Cohen, Huttner presented a workshop at the AAUW-Illinois Spring Convention. 42 people attended (including Penny Parish, Donna Sproston, and other women essential to the SWAN story), and as they watched *A Jury of Her Peers* together, the power of the film, combined with the subsequent discussion with filmmaker Sally Heckel, resonated with all who were there that day. AAUW-Illinois branches began inviting Huttner to come speak.

2004: At the summer planning meeting, President Kim Benziger and her AAUW-Illinois Board asked Huttner to provide updates for the Fall District Conferences, so "the project" needed a name. After weeks of brainstorming with input from over two dozen AAUW-Illinois members, everyone agreed: We were "**W**omen **i**n **t**he **A**udience **S**upporting **W**omen **A**rtists **N**ow!" The WITASWAN roll-out began at Illinois Valley Community College on October 2, 2004.

2005: Members of AAUW-Illinois (in collaboration with Chicago Area Women's History Council, Illinois Woman's Press Association and Women in the Director's Chair) invited filmmaker Sally Heckel back for a Silver Anniversary screening of *A Jury of Her Peers* at the Chicago Cultural Center on March 19, 2005 (timed to Women's History Month).

2006: Members of AAUW-Illinois (in collaboration with Illinois Woman's Press Association and the Australian Consulate-General Chicago) invited filmmaker Sarah Watt to screen her award-winning film *Look Both Ways* on March 18, 2006 (thus reinforcing Chicago's annual WITASWAN program tradition).

2007: In March, four Illinois organizations (Association for Women Journalists-Chicago, Illinois Woman's Press Association, International Women Associates, and Women in Film/Chicago) collaborated with AAUW-Illinois on the third annual WITASWAN program. The special guest was Felicia Middlebrooks, director of *Somebody's Child: The Redemption of Rwanda.*

2007: In April, AAUW-Illinois Program Vice President Lois Strom invited Martha Richards (Founder and Executive Director of WomenArts aka The Fund for Women Artists) to speak at Spring Convention about issues confronting women in the arts generally (beyond Huttner's film niche). Driving back to Chicago afterwards, Richards suggested broadening the WITASWAN mission to support for all women artists in every medium and Huttner immediately agreed.

2008: The first International SWAN Day was celebrated all around the world on Saturday, March 29. It was such a success that Richards and Huttner agreed to make it an annual event (to be held on the last Saturday of every March). The AAUW-Illinois Board issued a proclamation recognizing Huttner "for her creativity and her foresight."

2009: Women artists began working with wide variety of grassroots organizers to plan new SWAN Day events. WomenArts held a party introducing SWAN Day at the

Sundance Film Festival. Chilean novelist Isabel Allende made an inspiring SWAN Day video. The League of Professional Theatre Women organized a SWAN Day panel at Lincoln Center Library in Manhattan, and Chicago celebrated with special guest Nancy Savoca (winner of a Sundance Grand Jury Prize).

2010: Over 170 public events (plus many private events) were posted on WomenArts' online SWAN Day tracking calendar. In New York, Richards organized a sold-out panel discussion featuring feminist arts activists such as Elizabeth Sackler (Founder of the Sackler Center for Feminist Art at the Brooklyn Museum) and Carol Jenkins (Founding President of the Women's Media Center). In Chicago, six collaborating organizations welcomed Eileen Douglas for a screening of *My Grandfather's House*.

2011: In only four years, WomenArts has provided encouragement and collateral materials for over 700 International SWAN Day events all around the world including Argentina, Australia, Bosnia-Herzegovina, Bulgaria, Canada, China, Croatia, France, Germany, Ghana, India, Indonesia, Israel, Italy, Jamaica, Kenya, Philippines, Romania, Uruguay, Wales/U.K., and, of course, the USA.

Richards and Huttner (who now writes film reviews for the WomenArts website) are busily planning for the fifth annual International SWAN Day on March 31, 2012!

Become a Film Swan:

- See at least one film every month (preferably in a theatre) that was written and/or directed by a woman filmmaker.

- Explain the importance of WITASWAN to all of your friends, relatives, and acquaintances. And don't forget the men: Male support is critical too!

- Collaborate with local colleges, universities, and public libraries to sponsor an annual WITASWAN film series and/or start a WITASWAN movie club with your friends.

- Celebrate International SWAN Day on the last Saturday of every March ☺

Through our support for women filmmakers, we can redefine what consumers everywhere get to see on their movie screens.

In the words of Martha Lauzen:

"If we change media messages, we change the world."

Jan Lisa Huttner

Jan Lisa Huttner is an award-winning author/activist who writes regular columns as well as freelance articles for multiple print and internet outlets.

A member of AAUW Chicago, Inc. for over 25 years, Jan has served AAUW at branch, state, and national levels.

In 2004, she was asked to coordinate a new AAUW-Illinois project called WITASWAN ("wit-uh-swan"): **W**omen **i**n **t**he **A**udience **S**upporting **W**omen **A**rtists **N**ow! In 2008, these activities lead to the creation of International SWAN Day, now celebrated annually on the last Saturday of every March all around the world.

Jan received her B.A. from St. John's College in Annapolis, Maryland (the "Great Books" school), and Masters Degrees in Psychology from Harvard University and the University of Chicago. In addition to her commitment to AAUW, professional memberships include the Association for Women Journalists, the Chicago Film Critics Association, the Illinois Woman's Press Association/National Federation of Press Women, and the Women Film Critics Circle.

Photo Credit: Jennifer Girard

www.ingramcontent.com/pod-product-compliance
Lightning Source LLC
Chambersburg PA
CBHW060920040426
42445CB00011B/709